THE ART OF NEPAL

20. Avalokiteshvara. Ca. fourteenth century. H: 36″.

Prior to sending the image from the Golden Monastery in Patan, Nepal, to the exhibition, it was worshipped. Sindur (vermilion) powder was sprinkled on it to wish it a good journey.

The Art of Nepal

by Stella Kramrisch

Catalogue of the Exhibition presented under the Patronage of
His Majesty King Mahendra Bir Bikram Shah Deva

THE ASIA SOCIETY, INC. · Distributed by Harry N. Abrams, Inc.

THE ART OF NEPAL is the catalogue of an exhibition selected by Dr. Stella Kramrisch and shown in the Asia House Gallery in the summer of 1964 as an activity of the Asia Society, to further greater understanding and mutual appreciation between the United States and the peoples of Asia.

TABLE OF CONTENTS

FOREWORD

This catalogue seeks to record and interpret a first major exhibition of art from the ancient kingdom of Nepal. It is warmly hoped that its publication, like the display itself, will bring the creative genius of Nepal to new public knowledge and to a wider appreciation. The rare and beautiful examples of Nepali art that are being shown have been chosen by Dr. Stella Kramrisch who is the true author of this exhibition as well as of its catalogue. It is thanks to her extensive acquaintance with the culture of Nepal and to her distinguished scholarship in the entire field of Indic arts that the Asia House Gallery has been able to arrange the present display.

Dr. Kramrisch herein offers a pioneer statement regarding the historical development and the chronology of Nepali art. She shows, both in her text and by example, that the Newari people of Nepal created a native form and style of art, both for Hindu and Buddhist usage, that must be regarded as one of great originality, grace and power. Through Dr. Kramrisch's efforts a new chapter in the unfolding history of Asian art has, in fact, been sketched. This must be counted as a unique contribution to our continuing modern effort to know and understand the great cultures of the world.

The Asia House Gallery of the Asia Society is deeply grateful to the many courteous people and institutions who have aided us in preparing this exhibition and its catalogue. Our first indebtedness is to His Majesty the King of Nepal, King Mahendra Bir Bikram Shah Deva, who from the start of our enterprise promised to send several of the greatest treasures of his nation to the exhibition. We also extend thanks to the former Prime Minister, the Honorable Doctor Tulsi Giri, to former Ambassador of Nepal to the United States and to the United Nations, His Excellency Matrik Prasad Koirala, and to members of the Cabinet whose approval of our enterprise has made it possible to display several notable sculptures such as are not available outside of Nepal itself. In effecting this desirable arrangement, we have been most kindly aided by Sri Ramesh Jung Thapa, Director, and Sri Purna Harsha Bajracharya, Section Officer, His Majesty's Government, Ministry of Education, Department of Archaeology and Culture in Katmandu, as well as by our own Ambassador in Katmandu, the Honorable Henry E. Stebbins, by his Public Affairs Officer, Mr. Robert Jaffie, and by Mr. Nandaram Bhagut, whose assistance, extending far beyond the call of duty, has been invaluable to us.

It is thanks to the kind favor of the Government of India that we have obtained the several loans from this source, and to the solicitous concern of her Ambassador in Washington, His Excellency

B. K. Nehru, as well as to that of the Consul General in New York, Mr. Sunil K. Roy and his Consul Information, Mr. Z. L. Kaul. Similarly, we are grateful for the indefatigable spirit of helpfulness that is constantly displayed by Dr. Grace Morley, Director of the National Museum of New Delhi. As on earlier occasions, her assistance with loans from India has been crucial to our undertaking.

To Mr. Kumar Guha, Mr. Madan M. Rampal, and Mr. James J. O'Brien, Cargo Sales representatives with Pan American World Airways, we would express our heartiest thanks for their many helpful consultations and for their company's ready aid in transporting the shipments from Nepal.

On such an occasion, it is scarcely possible to thank with any adequacy the many lenders for their generosity in permitting loans from their collections. Happily, it is they who are the first to recognize the value of their cooperation and therefore seek to make our task the easier. We list their names elsewhere in this catalogue with our deepest appreciation. We feel certain that these lenders will also understand when they discover that in many instances the dates ascribed to their possessions, and their nomenclature, have been changed. These changes reflect Dr. Kramrisch's effort to re-chronicle the entire body of Nepali material as seen from the point of view of a total chronology.

Gordon B. Washburn
Director, Asia House Gallery

ACKNOWLEDGEMENTS

The author is greatly indebted to the Department of Archaeology and Culture of the Government of Nepal, to Sri Ramesh Jung Thapa, and Sri Purna Harsha Bajracharya, and to Sri D. M. Regmi. Dr. P. Pal has given invaluable and generous assistance in reading the inscriptions of several of the paintings and manuscripts. Mr. Gordon B. Washburn and Miss Virginia Field have revised the text with infinite patience. My warmest thanks go to H. E. Rishikesh Shaha.

Stella Kramrisch

LENDERS TO THE EXHIBITION

His Majesty the King Mahendra Bir Bikram Shah Deva, Patron of the Exhibition.

The Ashmolean Museum, Oxford, England.

Baroda Museum and Picture Gallery, Baroda, India.

Bharat Kala Bhavan, Banaras Hindu University, Banaras, India.

Mr. George P. Bickford, Cleveland, Ohio.

The British Museum, London, England.

The Brooklyn Museum, Brooklyn, New York.

Mr. and Mrs. Richard C. Bull, Philadelphia, Pennsylvania.

Cincinnati Art Museum, Cincinnati, Ohio.

The Cleveland Museum of Art, Cleveland, Ohio.

Collection of Nasli and Alice Heeramaneck

Dr. and Mrs. J. LeRoy Davidson, Los Angeles, California.

The Denver Art Museum, Denver, Colorado.

Department of Archaeology, Ministry of Education, His Majesty's Government,
   Katmandu, Nepal.

The Detroit Institute of Arts, Detroit, Michigan.

M. H. de Young Memorial Museum, San Francisco, California.

Dr. and Mrs. Samuel Eilenberg, New York City.

Mr. Donal Hord, San Diego, California.

Mr. Christmas Humphreys, London, England.

Mr. J. J. Klejman, New York City.

Stella Kramrisch

Mr. and Mrs. Aschwin Lippe, New York City.

The Metropolitan Museum of Art, New York City.

Musée Guimet, Paris, France.

Museum of Fine Arts, Boston, Massachusetts.

National Museum of India, New Delhi, India.

Nelson Gallery—Atkins Museum, Kansas City, Missouri.

The Newark Museum, Newark, New Jersey.

Mr. Alfonso A. Ossorio, East Hampton, L. I., New York.

Philadelphia Museum of Art, Philadelphia, Pennsylvania.

Mrs. James Marshall Plumer, Ann Arbor, Michigan.

Mrs. Sumitra Charat Ram, New Delhi, India.

Rijksmuseum voor Volkenkunde, Leiden, Holland.

Mr. E. M. Scratton, Oxford, England.

Seattle Art Museum, Seattle, Washington.

Stanford University Museum, Stanford, California.

Mrs. Edgar J. Stone, Toronto, Canada.

Mr. and Mrs. Erwin D. Swann, New York City.

Victoria and Albert Museum, London, England.

Mr. and Mrs. John W. Warrington, Cincinnati, Ohio.

William H. Wolff, Inc., New York City.

86. Mahakala, Protector of the Tent.   Pata.   Nepal school in Tibet.   Fifteenth century. $38^{1}/_{4}'' \times 26^{1}/_{4}''$.

INTRODUCTION

The ancient kingdom of Nepal, high in the Himalaya between India and Tibet, is a world of its own. This is how the people of Nepal think of themselves and of the origin of their country:

The legend tells — and facts prove — that where Nepal now is there once was a blue lake surrounded by snowclad mountains. They were the setting of its waters. No man could approach this lake. A Buddha of a former aeon, in his supreme knowledge and foreseeing the future destinies of Nepal, went on a pilgrimage to the lake and threw a lotus seed into its waters. A miraculous lotus arose and bloomed in the middle of the lake. A flame, purer and more splendid than the rays of the sun shot up from its center. This is how the Adi-Buddha, the Buddha from before all time, the self-existing one, was manifested directly in his essence.

Aeons passed. The Buddha of each aeon visited the lake. The Buddha of the third aeon prophesied that a Bodhisattva would come and cause land to appear above the waters.

Bodhisattva Manjusri, in the perfection of his wisdom, knew that Deity had spontaneously manifested on the waters of the lake. Manjusri left his home in faraway China, behind seven walls. From the north-east he entered the mountains around the lake and with his sword, "Moon-smile," he cut through the mountains. He cleft the rock and the imprisoned waters of the lake rushed through the gorge into the plains of India. This is how the river Vagmati came to be, and the road to India through the Pharping gorge in the Mahabharat range.

This is how the Buddhists of Nepal know of the origin of their country, whereas the Hindus of Nepal ascribe the same feat to Vishnu in his Krishna manifestation.

By their own myths the two great religions of Nepal convey the same inner experience of reality. They have their own gods with their specific shapes to which India had given names and form. They came to Nepal ready made, and Nepal infused them with the faith of its people so that the gods of Hinduism and Buddhism became identified with one another or assumed one another's qualities and attributes. Avalokiteshvara and Shiva coalesced in one image called Lokeshvara. To worship Buddha is to worship Shiva, says the Nepali *Mahatmya*, a text which guides the Brahman pilgrim through Nepal.

The sacred sites which the pilgrim visits are in the valley of Nepal, on the banks of its rivers, on the slopes and peaks of the low hills which once had been covered by the lake and where temples arose, and also in the towns with their sacred buildings, palaces and houses full of images.

The Nepal of art and legend is a small valley about 4,500 feet above sea level, eighteen miles long from east to west and twelve miles from north to south. Its people are the Newars. They are related to the other Mongoloid people of the entire country of Nepal, which extends about 500 miles along the central and eastern Himalaya and about 150 miles across. The people who live in the mountains are of Tibetan type whereas the Newars absorbed several waves of Indian immigrants. There is also a substratum of a race of Pre-Dravidians and Dravidians who were in Nepal even before the Newars.

The Newars however formed the bulk of the ancient inhabitants of the valley of Katmandu. It is they who created the art of Nepal, in close touch with that of India, preserving its traditions while evolving their own in the relative seclusion of the mountains and the separateness of their race.

Tradition speaks of a long association between Nepal and India. Buddha Shakyamuni was born in Lumbini, on the southern frontier of Nepal. He is said to have visited the valley of Nepal. It is also told of Emperor Ashoka (273—236 B. C.) that he came to the valley, caused stupas to be set up, and married his daughter to a Kshatrya of Nepal who founded Deo-Patan. She lived there and built a monastery and stupa near by, which to this day commemorates her name. The low, hemisperical shape of these so-called "stupas of Ashoka" corresponds to that of stupas set up in India at the time of Emperor Ashoka. So conscious or desirable was the association with Indian

rulers and nobility that the successive dynasties of ancient and mediaeval Nepal, the Licchavis and Mallas, carried or assumed the names of Indian clans and married Indian princesses.

Traders came from India in order to bring home the soft, pashmina wool blankets from Nepal. Buddhist monks joined the traders. This made the journey less hazardous. Buddhist refugees, in the course of history, found a haven in Nepal and there, about 300 B. C., the last great apostle of the Jains spent the final years of his life. All this is reported by Indian sources. They do not say when the images of Indian gods came to Nepal.

The shapes in which the Newars venerated their own divinities, which had preceded the gods of Buddhism and Hinduism in Nepal, sharply differed from the forms of the latter. Stones were venerated in their natural shapes, whether singly, piled in heaps under trees, raised on altars or still in the ground below the surface of the earth. Such *objets trouvés* were numerous but they did not arouse the visual imagination, did not clamor for precise limits, proportion, or similarity to anything. Only when the gods of India in their Indian form came to Nepal did the history of Nepali art begin. The numinous stones are formless and timeless. They are worshipped to this day.

The art of Nepal not only became famous in itself but also played an initiatory and decisive part in the art of Tibet and of China. Hsüan Tsang, the Chinese monk who went to India

I. Vishnu Vikranta Murti.   467 A. D.   Pashupati, Nepal.

17

and left the most informative and dependable account of the sites that he visited and the places at which he stayed, did not go to Nepal, but heard of the country from monks whom he met during his two-year stay in Nalanda, or who accompanied him on his way from Ayodhya to Vaishali. What Hsüan Tsang transmitted to posterity is not flattering to Nepal. His informants do not seem to have enjoyed their stay in this cold and alien valley. Even so, they could not fail to be struck by the "skill and facility in the arts" of the Nepalis. This, coming from Buddhist monks accustomed to the splendors of painting and sculpture in the monasteries of India, at Ajanta, Nalanda, and elsewhere, is not to be underrated. They also saw that then, as to this day, "monasteries and temples of gods are contiguous," although Katmandu, Patan, and Bhatgaon, the three great cities of the valley, had not yet been founded when Hsüan Tsang wrote about his travels in the second quarter of the seventh century A. D.

It was at this time that Tibet, the other neighbor country of Nepal, became a great power due to the genius of Emperor Srong-tsan-gampo. After a victory over Nepal, legend tells, he asked for the hand of Princess Bri-btsum, the daughter of King Amshuvarman of Nepal. She is said to have brought with her from Nepal, when the bridal party went to Tibet, a miraculous sandalwood statue of Tara and also a begging bowl of lapis lazuli that once had belonged to Lord Buddha himself. Srong-tsan-gampo also defeated the Emperor of China and married a T'ang princess, as ardent a Buddhist as Princess Bri-btsum. The two queens who brought Buddhism to Tibet are venerated as incarnations of the green and the white Tara. Princess Bri-btsum, the incarnation of the green Tara, symbolic of the role Nepal was to play in Tibetan art, was first in bringing the gods and treasures of her country to Tibet where she was joined by the Chinese Princess Wen-cheng.

This extension of the art of Nepal came about around the year 640(?). Art in Nepal of the seventh century left an indelible impression not only in Tibet but on those who visited Nepal from India and China. In the middle of the seventh century (657) the Chinese envoy Wang Hsüan Ts'e described the manifold wonders which he saw in Nepal. There was a lake which was on fire. The King of Nepal told the envoy that there was a golden casket in the lake. It appeared but was submerged when anyone wanted to take it. Its gold was the gold of the diadem of the Bodhisattva Maitreya, the future Buddha. It was guarded by the Fire-Serpent.

Leaving aside the symbolic meaning of the story told by King Narendra Deva (640—680?) to the Chinese envoy, the golden diadem of Maitreya must be imagined as similar to those which Bodhisattvas and gods are seen to wear in their images in stone and metal. Some of these were set with precious stones. Precious stones also decorated the buildings. The T'ang annals, based on the account of Wang Hsüan Ts'e, describe the royal palace of Nepal as having

II. Vishnu Vikranta Murti .   476 A. D.   Lajampat, Katmandu, Nepal (now in the Bir Library, Katmandu).

a central tower of seven stories. Its metal work, balustrades, screens, columns, and beams were decorated with precious stones. Neither the number of stories nor the decoration of the towering structure appear to have been exaggerated. This structure was, no doubt, built in the Indian tradition. In India, the many-storied temple towers in stone bear witness to this day to the comparable wooden structures, long since perished, of which they were adaptations. The wooden houses with painted wooden sculptures in Deo-Patan, the capital of Nepal, were a reflection of the splendor of the palace. Wang Hsüan Ts'e himself describes temples of many stories on an isolated mountain near the capital. He also marvels at a similar broadly terraced structure in the capital, 200 feet (*ch'ih*) high and 400 feet around, with wondrous sculptures in its four pavilions. They were adorned with precious stones and pearls.

To decorate metal sculptures with precious stones is neither decadent, "late", nor barbaric. The mellow and deep glow of cabochon-cut spinel rubies, the blue freshness of turquoise, the light of rock crystal, and the gleam of the pearl exceed in effect the inlaying of metal with metal, as of bronze with gold, silver, or copper, which are seen in Indian and Nepali metal images of the seventh century. Polychromy, not only by means of pigments made from stones and metals but by the original substances, is part of the sculpture of Nepal. This must have astonished the Chinese envoy in the seventh century, much as it does Western taste today.

Centuries later, when there was no direct contact between the King of Nepal and the Mongol court of China, it was the art of Nepal which penetrated into China and Tibet. It is said that in all the monasteries of both countries most of the images were the work of A-ni-ko.

A-ni-ko (1244—1306), a descendant of the royal family of Nepal, was so accomplished an artist and worker in metal that in 1260, in spite of his youth, he headed a contingent of eighty artists from Nepal whom King Jayabhimadeva had summoned when P'ags-pa, abbot of the Saskya monastery in Tibet and spiritual advisor of Kublai Khan, was ordered by the latter to erect a golden stupa in Tibet. This task was carried out so successfully that the abbot persuaded A-ni-ko to follow him to China where he entered the service of Kublai Khan. By 1274 he was in charge of all metal workers, and he also painted portraits on silk of the Yüan emperors. Four years later he was appointed controller of the Imperial studios. Among his titles, when he died, was that of Duke of Liang. His chief pupil was the Chinese, Lin Yüan. The tradition which A-ni-ko had created in Tibet and China lasted for a long time, not only in metal and clay, but also in lacquer. Moreover, it was kept alive, by new contacts, into the eighteenth century (71).

It seems a long way from the formless stones indicative of the presence of divinity (*dyu*) to the accomplished work of A-ni-ko. But the passage of time has not affected belief in the validity and the efficacy of the unhewn stones.

To this day they may be placed and worshipped side by side with a carved stone or gold-plated metal image of any phase of image making. The four Buddhist goddesses, consorts of the Buddhas of the four directions, are represented by simple stones on the southern stupa of Patan. Such co-existence maintains a tension between the form that is the work of art, on the one hand, and the unformed datum of nature, the mere support of the numinous, on the other.

The range of the sculptures and paintings of Nepal is from the figurative to the abstraction of the mandala, the geometrically ordered paint-ing (87). The figures of Buddhist art, whether shown at peace or in frenzy, have their definite place in the intelligible structure of Buddhist thought or in the visible field of a mandala, an instrument and diagram for obtaining spiritual reintegration.

The images of the gods came from India, together with the theory and techniques of their manufacture. However, the rough and unhewn stones, supports of the numinous, belonged to the earth of Nepal which once upon a time was covered by a lake. Finally they had become exposed, ready to attract the attention and awe of a herdsman as he wandered along or mused while tending his flock.

The valley of Nepal came into existence in an aeon long past, in mythical time. Its fertile soil was covered by dense vegetation. None dared to interfere with its luxuriance until one day the soil was opened for agriculture. This event is assigned to the reign of Vrishadeva, the great grandfather of King Manadeva.[1] The latter dedi-cated two images of Vishnu Vikranta (I and II) and set up many stone slabs, and had them covered with inscriptions and with reliefs.

The transition from a pastoral mode of life to an agricultural one, and from an unhewn stone to the complex organization of the relief of a stele or sculpture in the round, is rapid. Yet again, time is of no consequence when a people, receptive of a fully evolved art like that of India, becomes identified with the religious experience that the form of this art expresses. Nor is it necessary to take literally the span of four genera-tions from Vrishadeva to Manadeva, although they are historically accountable figures. Its short duration denotes a rapid and total change, just as in the opposite sense the aeons, when the former Buddhas came and went their way, denote an incalculable time, before years began to count, a rhythmical time of inner experience which attunes the inner attitude of the believer to all that happens.

This rapid change from one mode of life to an-other and the first making of a self-portrait by an artist coincide in the legend of Balbala who lived in the reign of Vrishadeva. Before him, none had dared to lay open the earth for agriculture. Balbala the "stutterer" did it. He had no family, none to mourn or to remember him. Before he died he set up with his own hands a statue of himself. This statue became the center of a cult.

Balbala, stigmatized by his defect of speech and lack of a family, was destined for the "hubris,"

III. Pilgrims in the Mountains. Near Kathesimbhu, Katmandu, Nepal. Ca. seventh century. (The chronology of Indian art of the sixth to eighth centuries, on which the style of the Nepali sculptures is based, is not as yet securely established.)

the daring crime, of violating mother earth. He dug into her and became the first agriculturist; he cut into the stone and in his hubris made a statue, not of a god, but of himself. For these acts of cultivation and creation, he became the center of a cult. His hubris, and the handicaps which predestined him for it, were cancelled and outweighed by his work. Balbala, hero of agriculture and art, belongs entirely to Nepal. Daring and self-assertive, he converts his stigma into

his glory by having given to the country the cultivation of its ground and the art of portraiture—the latter through the equivocal achievement of self-consciousness.

This altogether un-Indian legend is told in one breath together with other memorable happenings that took place in the reign of King Vrishadeva. Just as his ancestors had done, so also did this king set up images of the Buddhas and of Lokeshvara. The revolution brought about by the "stutterer" is carried along in the flux of the narrative.

The two relief steles (dated 467) of the time of Manadeva, fourth in succession from Vrishadeva, are images of Vishnu (I and II). No Buddhist image can be assigned to his age.[2] One statue preceding the dated images of Manadeva's reign appears to be that of a king (1). Portrait statues have their place in Indian art, the grandiose finesse of the statue of the Kushana Emperor Kanishka of the first century A. D. makes it one of the great works of Indian sculpture.

Portraits of kings appear on Indian Kushana coins found in Nepal.[3] The "statue of a king" (1) from Mrigasthali, Pashupati, has, however, a physiognomy of pure Nepali form. Nimbate and diademmed, it exhibits cruelty in the serene vaults which span from ear to ear and bind the features of the face to the broad dome of the forehead. Wide shoulders and chest, malleably modeled, lead to the disciplined flatness of the abdomen, and to the fulness of the drapery which sets off this part of the body as the halo does the face. The retracted elbows make the gesture of the arms instantaneous. The hands have just been placed on the lateral bows of the shawl. An economy of ornament and costume underscores the modeled planes of the figure. Its physiognomy is Mongoloid, and more childlike, but as determined, as are kings' faces in pre-Khmer sculpture.

The width of Vishnu's stride (I and II), the oblique sweep of the legs stretched in one ascending line, is as determined as are the stance and physiognomy of the king. Although the self-same moment of the myth is shown in both the reliefs (I and II) and with the self-same actors and a similar disposition of their figures, the identity of the date, the year 467, of these two carvings is revealed by their inscriptions and not by their styles. The one tablet (I) with its squat, uncouth, and cubically separate figures, differs greatly from the other (II), which is elegant in the composition of the figures and the flux of their contours. A detail of costume stands out, the high three peaked crown, its volume widening toward the top.

During the fifth and sixth centuries the contacts of Nepal were with the Indian schools of sculpture in Mathura and central India. Whether Indian sculptors from these centers taught in Nepal, or Nepali sculptors came to India to work under Indian masters, or whether sculptures reached Nepal in that period cannot be answered at present.

Traits of these several Indian schools mingled in Nepal, but whichever components prevail they are subsumed to a whole which is Nepali. Its form is harder, the line more consciously drawn. Watchfully, daintily, and with firmness the sculptor has groomed his presentation. These qualities become its backbone and content. The "king" from Mrigasthali, Pashupati, embodies this content in a style corresponding to Gupta sculptures of the early fifth century.

The statue of Devi (Gauri or Tara) (2) in her compactness represents this sculptural conception about two centuries later. The three-dimensional ponderosity of the figure makes it appear saturated and gravid with its own presence. When a figure is that of a god or goddess its divinity is embodied in fulsome clarity. When it is that of a king his status and character inform the tension of the curved planes of the figure. Straightforward and compact, these sculptured presences stand firm. Their solidity has absorbed into itself the Indian tradition of modeling which follows the movement of the breath and the ebb and surge of the sap of life, the vital process itself, caught in its course. All this, as an achieved form in Indian sculpture, is as thoroughly understood by the Nepali sculptor as is a Buddhist sacred text by its Nepali expositor. To him the oscillating curves of Indian form are the substance in which he works, so that the sculpture stands solid and is established in the surge of its curves and the palpitations of its planes. The static form grips the swelling, vaulted shapes replete with an inner movement, and subordinates them to the firmness of its discipline.

Whether carved in stone or cast in solid metal (3), the sculptures made in the two centuries of ever-renewed contacts with India show that more than one school of Indian sculpture provoked their form. In the fifth to sixth centuries the impulse once given by the school of Mathura was still felt and the Gupta schools of central India contributed their part; other Indian centers become palpable solely in the effect they had on Nepali sculpture, their work not being preserved.

By the seventh century, the Deccan and Western India had contributed their tradition. The work of the Nepali sculptor has some features in common with that of the Aurangabad cave sculptures and of the Western school centered in North Gujarat (Samalajī), and, nearer to Nepal, with that of Uttar Pradesh with the temple at Deogarh, and of Bihar, where the new "post-Gupta" style produced monuments like the Varaha Avatar in Aphsar. Nepal was in direct touch with the vital currents of Indian art.

Another component of Nepali sculptural form is a sober appraisal of the roundness and the rhythms of the contour and also of the countenance of the figure (III). With this goes a loving presentation of children and flowers. In the art of the whole of Indian Asia, Nepali sculpture has created an image of childhood in many figures of nameless children, whose movements are pristine as those of animals when they know themselves to be unobserved. The flying Vidyadharas in Nepali sculpture are not valiant youths of charismatic appeal, nor the flying Devatas angelic, or gnome-like as they are in Indian reliefs. They are Devaputras, children of heaven, who know how to fly. In Nepali sculpture the god-child Krishna, child-hero who vanquishes the serpent (IV), is only a few years old, not yet a lad as Indian sculpture shows him. His small-featured face is thoroughly Nepali. There is a streak of cruelty in his triumphant elation, the same cruelty that rules over the lineaments of the king's countenance in the statue from Mrigasthali, Pashupati (1). Nor is it

IV. Krishna subjugates the serpent Kaliya.　Old Palace, Katmandu, Nepal.　Ca. seventh century.

absent from the delicate beauty of goddesses. In some of their images seemingly incompatible components of the Nepali style interpenetrate just as they do in images of the Bodhisattvas (V). They are sumptuous in the almost physical impact of their presence, insinuating in their fleshliness and at the same time beyond reach in their detachment or in the bliss of absorption which their faces show. Ambiguously both sleek and stern in their luxuriance and detachment, the sculptures of the early seventh century, whether Hindu or Buddhist, excel in a gemlike precision of surface finish and in the definition of detail.

These details are of diverse provenance. Among them are the voluminous masses of pleated garment, oblivious of the classically Western folds whence they derive their bulk and arrangement (2); taut, vaulting planes of carved volumes (of Indian provenance) incised or inlaid with the geometrical figures of patterned textiles which cling to them (3, 4); crowns of mitre shape and others which, covered with delicate relief, widen as they ascend in three detached crests from the forehead. The coiffures range from Gupta-type wigs (III), their profusion of locks like a shower of pearls, to braided arrangements placed on top of the head or laterally, all known to India but in Nepal as much stereotyped as they are intricately described. Even more varied is the attitude toward jewelry; simple shapes such as pearl strings with a central gem or "rosette" (V, 5) and large, flat, circular or "rosette" shaped earrings are shown in the seventh century; three-dimensional *amalaka* shapes are particularly conspicuous in earlier times, and intricate designs are common after the eighth century. All these ornaments are worn in their established places near the joints of limbs and body as in Indian sculpture; or sometimes they are absent, leaving body and limbs free from their magic protection and also from accentuation and encumbrance, so that their kneaded, modeled volumes have no ornament but their own smooth surfaces.

In this freedom of choice Nepali sculpture avails itself of the resources of India and of its own tradition as it gathers momentum from one work to the other. Confirmed in its own ways, a local tradition tests its strength against the inflowing Indian types. Transplanted into the body of Nepali art, their cumulative combinations and exchanges are part of its substance and are transformed with it, while one or the other motif is carried along as a residual shape in a new context. Eclecticism and conscious borrowing are part of this process.

The art of Nepal is not a regional school of Indian art. It is on the receiving end of a one way traffic. No art forms flow from Nepal to India; they stay in the mountain kingdom having received the impress of their makers, the Newars. Whatever admixture of Indian blood the Newar craftsman possesses makes for this readiness to absorb the traditions of the Indian schools, but his creative use of them is to the credit of the Newar element itself. It is as unmistakable in the form of the sculptures as it is in the physiognomies of their figures.

These figures, if they are not carved against a plain ground, are set against or ensconced in rugged, cubistic configurations (III). These represent rocks and symbolize nature. Their patterns had evolved in India through half a millennium and more, from Barhut on, before they reached the mountains of Nepal and there proliferated. No new mode of showing mountains, the natural setting of Nepal, entered their closely textured patterns. Nepali art transformed the physiognomy of the figure of man from an ideal Indian to an ideal Nepali type, but did not, before the eighteenth century, look up from traditional Indian practice and formula and coin a version of its own experience of surrounding nature. The Newari sculptor, in his intention, remained true to the Indian original. A power stronger than this conscious aim wrought the transformation of the human figure and its modeling according to his own physiognomy and his own way of looking, feeling, and forming. But it is not his full-blooded self, moved in its utmost depth, to which he has recourse. Groomed and dainty, his figures exist in a world of elegance and etiquette, even where their form is akin to and contemporary with Deccani cave sculptures like those of Aurangabad.

Because of this inner distance from primary and artistically creative religious experience and the consciously conducted, cultivated line which circumscribes it, Nepali sculptures from the second half of the seventh century anticipate some of the character of the later Pala sculptures of eastern India. To the first half of that century may be ascribed some of the most relevant sculptures of Nepal (III, IV; 2—4).

The images of Buddha and of the Bodhisattvas Padmapani (V) and Vajrapani carved between pilasters in niches facing the four directions, on a prismatic pedestal supporting a stupa at the Henakarna Mahavihara (or Dhvaka Baha) in Katmandu (ca. seventh century) are closely related, in their architectural setting, to the Dashavatar Temple in Deogarh in Uttar Pradesh, India. This temple is assignable to about 600 A. D. or the end of the sixth century. The modeling of its figures is more detailed, more relaxed than that of the Nepali images, relying as it does on the knowledge of Gupta sculpture of the sixth century, whereas that of the images of the *Licchavi Chaitya* (as a stupa of this kind is commonly called in Nepal) of the Dhvaka Baha is summary. It suppresses detail in order to strengthen the purity of the contour. Within it, the figure has filled out, shoulders and thighs are more rounded, the stone having become the flesh of a conception of might. It surges in vaulted planes of immaculate precision whose intersections are as neat as those of clover leaves. This summation and precision are the work of the Newari sculptor. Actually Indian sculpture at that moment was moving in the same direction, away from the tender sensibility of Gupta form to a heightened sense of simplified volume. Sculptures from Aphsar,

V. Bodhisattva
Padmapani.
Dhvaka Baha,
Katmandu,
Nepal.
Ca. seventh century.

Bihar, of the reign of Adityasena would be the next Indian reference along the arrow of time. They appear to be about a generation later than the Dhvaka Baha sculptures, being one step further away from Gupta finesse.

The clearing of descriptive detail from the contour, the emphasis on its harmonious amplitude, are the outcome of the consideration which the Newar sculptor gives to the Gupta style of Northern India. If the curved planes tend to become satin smooth, the spacing of belts, ornaments, and sashes calculated, the flutter of reed-like folds arranged, they are part of the Nepali style.

In its treatment of the sculptural mass, this style contributed two essential types of form, the one endowed with movement, the other with a balance compacted of movement. The movement is that of a serpentine writhing and is embodied in the shape of the serpent (IV), or in a lotus stalk (V) or in limbs of the human shape (1). The former type, endowed with movement, culminates in the body of the heroic child-god Krishna (IV), an interlacing in space of serpentine volumes, gyrating and charged with a power of resilience whose modifications are incorporated in the body of the Naga King and in his serpent hoods.[4] When, however, the figure is shown at rest, compacted of movement, as is the image of Gauri (2), firmly planted on her feet, the figure is filled like an amphora with a movement that expands from the core of every limb and of each part of the body, until it sets up its limits, which are the shape itself of that limb or part. It is in this way that the glorious opulence of the legs of the goddess has come about, the firm arcs of their contour, the purity of its transition to the erect torso which this contour carries upward like a chalice. The rib-cage here serves as a stem, its flatness as a zone of contrast and transition to the round volumes above.

A counterpoint to these ascending sinuous volumes is formed by the angular shapes of the descending, draped, upper garment slung around the shoulder. The zigzag pattern of its pleated ends, forming triangles in space, is as calculated as is the flatness of the garment where it clings to the shoulder. The volume of this upper garment on the proper left of the figure is repeated by the slighter vertical masses of the folds in which the diaphanous skirt is gathered, between and beside the legs, squaring their rotundities. Foliate scrolls and creepers, in low relief and in compartments of their own, frame the lower part of the image. The elegant geometrical dovetailing of foliate scroll and pleated garment is given a less arresting version in the image of Padmapani at the Dhvaka Baha (V).

To these stone sculptures may be added a metal image of the goddess (3) standing on a lotus pedestal (*mahambhujapitha*). Both feet planted on its seedpod, with a bend in the hip, the goddess allows her left arm to follow the curve of this stance, holding the left hand (in *kapittha-hasta*) against her thigh whereas her right hand, pointing downward on the retracted hip, bestows gifts from her open palm. The upper garment here is drawn across her body, front and back, and falls behind her left arm in a sequence of pleated folds whose concave plane curves away from the body, augmenting the lateral projections of the skirt. From below the ornament of the belt, folds stream down as if from a separate sash. They follow the curve of the stance. The narrow, sloping shoulders are loaded with ornaments. The crests of beaded armlets reach up to them as they do in the image of Vishnu Anantashayin, in Deogarh. Flower-shaped earrings rest on the shoulders and cover a double strand bead necklace, broadening and solidifying the transition from the face to the body, so that body, face, and crown form one sculptural unit whose mass is surmounted by the forward tilt of the halo. It rises from behind the shoulders and leans on the lateral meshes of the coiffure and the crest of the diadem of the goddess. This mighty coiffure broadens the solid figure; its height is augmented by the pointed halo of flames.

Bounded by flat waves of hair, held in place by a flat band of the diadem, the oval face of the goddess is of a pure Nepali type whose family likeness with the countenance of the child-god Krishna is unmistakable. The metal image of the goddess goes further in its stylizations of the face. High, arched brows are incised above the meeting of the planes of forehead and lids, adding an overtone of wonder and increasing the Mongoloid character of her mien. This is indicated by the incised line of the upper eyelids which runs closely

parallel with their elongated curve, shielding the almond-shaped eyes. It suggests the fold of the upper lid; it descends to the inner corner of the eye though it does not cover it. The Nepali goddess has her counterparts in the rock-cut goddesses of Aurangabad whose maternal amplitude her shape emulates.

The image is solidly cast in copper which has apparently a considerable admixture of gold. Shawl and skirt are inlaid with gold and silver stripes and circles. The circles have holes in their centers and around each a square is outlined by incised pinpoint dots which give the effect of a woven or *ikat*-dyed pattern. The gems in all the ornaments are cast in metal whereas the eight-petaled flower in the center of the girdle now shows an empty cavity in the center. It would have been inlaid with gold or silver or with a precious stone.

The halo, oval inside and pointed outside, has two plain inner borders whereas the broad, outer rim consists of bifurcated flames increasing in size toward the central peak marked by a plain oval. The halo and the long end of the upper garment were made separately in the wax model as thick flat shapes; they were affixed to the figure and then cast together with it. In the back view their curved surfaces are echoed in the skirt which, similarly flattened, flares out in an irregular trapezium shape. This flattened, abstract treatment of the back of the image, particularly of the skirt, is reminiscent of very ancient Indian precedents seen in the colossal Yaksha and Yakshini

VI. Vishnu Sridhara.
Changu Narayan,
Nepal.
Ca. ninth century.

figures from Didarganj and Patna, of Mauryan date.

The feet of Gauri appear tied to the ground by the heavy bands of the anklets, which skirt the ground as they pass around the heels. The single petals of the base with their broad, simple shapes agree with other simplifications peculiar to this image, such as the flat and bent section of folds or the solid rim of abstract flames. In the lower half of the pedestal, with its double row of petals turned downward, no petals are shown at the back. A related image of the goddess is richer in its modeling but its countenance is less pronouncedly Nepali (4).

More exaggerated than in the stone fragment (2) is the slim high waist, holding up her large, closely-set breasts. They are modeled as they surge from the chest as are those of the woman in the stone relief (III). This relief shows a flower-offering scene in the mountains within a three dimensional, synthetically cubistic setting equivalent to those painted in Cave II, Ajanta.

At present the existence of "early" Nepali metal images is not recognized. The fact that some of them are gilded and others, after the eighth century, are also encrusted with jewels, and that this technique is not known from extant examples in India prior to the later Pala period, supports this view. But the argument is weak and is contradicted by the testimony of Wang Hsüan Ts'e, the Chinese envoy who described Nepali architecture and sculpture.

The early part of the seventh century in Nepal and India was one of great sculptural achievement. In Nepal, the reign of Amshuvarman was propitious. Hsüan Tsang, the Chinese pilgrim to India, who knew about Nepal from hearsay only, extols King Amshuvarman who had ruled "with sound knowledge and sagacity of spirit." Justly famous, he created an atmosphere which must have stimulated all the arts. He was at first a high feudatory" or *Mahasamanta* of King Shivadeva who ruled from 575 to 617. Amshuvarman is said to have become the Regent in 602. He died between 615—620.

The wealth of sculptural invention in the early part of the seventh century was to remain a storehouse for the next half millennium of Nepali sculpture.

From the middle of the seventh century and its second half, Hinduism as well as Buddhism set up cult images in which the figure of the main deity, by its size and central position, dominates two minor images (VI, VII, VIII). The most frequent Hindu type is that of Vishnu accompanied by the standing figures of Lakshmi and Garuda, whereas Padmapani Avalokiteshvara is the main figure in the Buddhist configuration. Padmapani is accompanied by two kneeling nimbate and worshipping female figures. The image of Vishnu Sridhara at Changu Narayan is representative of the first type (VI). The completeness of its iconography coupled with the rigidity of its form suggest a later date, but in none of its motifs and idioms are this and allied images derived from Pala steles of Vishnu of the ninth and tenth centuries. The Vishnu image at Changu Narayan is literally a configuration of three separate images, each on a pedestal of its own, assembled in front of an ornamental broad rim of a stele. The stele has the appearance of being translated into stone from three bronze images cast in the round and placed in front of a *prabha-mandala* in repoussé technique.

The lotus pedestal of Lakshmi is circular and the rock base of Garuda is transformed to a circle. Lotus bases and flame edges of halos and mandorlas of the seventh century were elaborated in different designs, of single, double, and triple units of flames or petals, in planar or more full-bodied patterns, the simple curved plane of the lotus petal occurring also in a later phase. The rock cubes of Garuda's pedestal with the two-tiered, circular section form a three-dimensional pattern in black and white, the underside of each tier being cut obliquely. This ingenious adaptation to the shape of the lotus base strengthens the formal structure of the stele, making the two lateral figures supporting pillars to Vishnu's stance. They are also attached to him in width, by the interlocking of fluttering shawls, cape-like wings, and lotus plants resulting in excited arabesques to which neither the stolid modeling of the figures nor the symmetry of the stele respond. Only the claw-like scrolls and tremulous leaves of the "vase of plenty" on the front panel of Vishnu's pedestal express this agitation. No "vase of plenty" (*purna-ghata*) in Indian sculpture brims

with such tortured fragments, though their style is derived from work of the later part of the seventh and the eighth centuries when Elura, Alampur (Svarga Brahma Temple, 681) and the early temples in Bhuvaneshwar, Orissa, offer parallels in the stylization of the scroll.

The image of Lakshmi (VI) though related to that of the metal statuette of Gauri (3), differs from her by its unsuccessful integration of jewelry and headdress with the figure, by a condensation of the opulent sweep of the body between knees and waist (in the image of Gauri this sweep extended down to the knees), and by the comparatively small breasts which appear more as if set on to the chest than springing from it. The unified sculptural volume of the image of Gauri, exaggeratedly shown by her left arm almost without elbow—all of one piece like a serpent's body—is here replaced by an articulation not only of elbows and knees but also of the thorax against the abdomen. With this greater flexibility in the joints the face is held less erect, it looks down on, rather than confronts, the devotee.

The fleshy, short-featured, broad face of Vishnu (VI) appears as Indian as it is Nepali. As in the metal figurine of Gauri, high arches are incised in one thin line above the modeled ridge of the brows. They descend in a point to the root of the nose. The small and puppet-like mouth is common to all three figures. The arms raised from the elbows have a bulging contour between elbow and wrist, a mannerism that came to stay in Nepali sculpture. Discus and club, the weapons

VII. Padmapani
Avalokiteshvara.
Near Yampi Baha,
Patan, Nepal.
End of seventh
or early eighth
century.

of the god, are given prominence by their size, whereas his cosmic symbols held in his lower hands are small, the conch held horizontally, the lotus dwindled to a small bud.

Here the crown of Vishnu is a high shape attached to the head by a beaded diadem whence arises a mass of pleated, stiff material decorated with three circles of the goldsmith's art, the frontal one encompassing a leonine face of glory (*kirtti-mukha*). The figure of Vishnu is segmented by its jewelry and apparel, among which the long sacred thread passes from the left shoulder underneath the waistbelt, above the folded upper garment. The latter is fastened to the waistbelt and draped in a loop across the thighs. The sacred thread is tucked in near the right thigh then falls nearly to the knee. With their tubular folds and the three-dimensional pattern of their edges, the ends of the upper garment contribute to the complexity of the stele in its lower part. The striped and patterned loincloth, worn short on the left leg and long on the right, is gathered between the legs and preserves the zigzag pattern of the drapery of classical Western art.

The image of Garuda, similarly attired but wearing a cape of wings, a serpent around the neck, two different earrings and a coiffure peculiar to Garuda images in Nepal, stands with a slight flexion in an attitude of veneration. The draped end of the dhoti clings to the right leg, leaving the left one free.

The image of Padmapani near the Yampi Baha in Patan (VII) is without the dreary solemnity of the Vishnu image. It is imbued with a harmonious warmth of figures, ground and spacing. The three lotus pedestals are combined into one base for the total image. The scroll of the broad rim is utterly conventional. The young, short, sturdy figure of Padmapani Avalokiteshvara is without a waistbelt; nothing breaks the continuity of the contour. Held against the image at the Dhvaka Baha (V) the modeling has become tired, the thighs sag and the legs are wooden. Zest, however, comes from right and left, from the impetuous kneeling and greeting by the two royal ladies. A new experience here has infused a traditional motif (V) of Indian Gupta origin with the immediacy of its meaning.[5]

The posture of the two kneeling figures amplifies the sacred space which the recessed ground around Avalokiteshvara indicates. The precision of their shapes accords with the immediacy of the movement, and a return may be noted to the modeling of the bust as in the earlier sculptures. If the necklaces seem to indicate a new fashion (shared by the image of Tara [No. 1948, 2—18, 1] in the British Museum), the armlets with their high crest in the old style reach up to the shoulders; they are placed higher than those of Avalokiteshvara. His beautiful face, full of compassion, belongs to the family of the Vishnu image. It has none of the rapt bliss of self-absorption of the Gupta-like Dhvaka Bodhisattva.

The sculptors chose for their images many different combinations and variations of motifs, however standardized their main features were becoming. Motifs in common, such as the crown of whatever shape, widening towards the top, or the long and tucked-in sacred thread are differently treated according to the sensitivity of the sculptor. It is of a high order as shown by the sacred thread of the image of Avalokiteshvara where its beaded string accompanies, caresses and accentuates the modeling.

Related to this stone image of Padmapani Avalokiteshvara (VII) though more powerful and consistent in its modeling and structure, is the gilded copper figure of Vajrapani in the Stanford University Museum, California (5).[6] Technically, it has the affixed halo in common with the image of Gauri and also the abbreviation and compression of the drapery into a thick metal sheet flaring away from the figure, as is seen in the back view. The left arm of Bodhisattva Vajrapani, though somewhat more modeled and bent in the elbow, parallels that of Gauri. In the proportion of its body the statuette resembles the stone carving of Avalokiteshvara, but is more unified in its relation of body and legs; the thighs do not sag; the simplification of the end of the dhoti into a curved sheet leaves, as in the image of Avalokiteshvara, an interval beside the left leg, strengthening its silhouette. This idiom is also seen in the figures of Vishnu and Garuda.

By its width of face at the side of the cheek bones, and its short features, the countenance of Vajrapani belongs to the conventions of Nepali sculpture, though the nose is more Indian, being prominent. Above the modeled brows is the thin, incised line forming an angle at the root of the nose. The ornaments in relation to the body are as conspicuous as those of Vishnu. Their contact with the body lacks, however, the finesse of the image of Padmapani.

Another, larger image of Padmapani at the Srighata Mahavihara or Sigha Baha, Kathesimbhu, Katmandu (VIII) concludes the series of "early" Bodhisattva images, that is prior to circa 800 A. D. Contrasting with the ponderosity of the figures in the seventh century, is the attenuation of the image and its halting contour. The latter is even more conspicuous in the lower half of the image than it had been in Fig. VII. In the upper part of his body, the Padmapani at Kathesimbhu rises, under a new disposition of form, above the hesitations in the treatment of the lower part. The figure has the precision of curved metal sheets. In its elongation, this Nepali Bodhisattva image is reminiscent of some colossal stone Bodhisattvas from northern Orissa.

The face, similar to the torso, is pure in its linear definition, following as it does the model of the ideal Nepali type. The raised ridge of the brow, having dispensed with the incised line along it, now meets at an angle at the root of the nose. The Newar eye is indicated by an incised line parallel and close to the edge of the lowered, upper lid of doubly curved bow shape. The lips, relaxed in their schematic beauty, have left behind the many shapes given to them before. In its mask-like perfection, this formalized face is yet reminiscent of that of the god-child Krishna.

At the base of the slab, the three lotus blooms here belong to one plant and are held aloft by the stem and its ramifications. This motif carries here a "double lotus" in the middle, the pedestal of the main divinity, and two artichoke-like "single lotuses" on which are enthroned the royal women devotees, dwarfed and lumped versions of those of the Padmapani in Patan (VII). The right hand of the Bodhisattva in both the steles rests on a lotus support, akin to the florid shape in the Vishnu stele (VI).

The lower part of the stele does not share the clarity of its upper half and some of its stodginess recurs in the heavy-handed, pedantic detail in the elaboration of the crown and the lotus flower. The central crest of the crown, a flame-edged niche arising from a lotus, enshrines the image of Buddha Amitabha, the spiritual father of the Bodhisattva. The flames here have stems which curl up at the ends.

Similar flames surround the lotus-discus (*cakra*) of a gold-plated metal image of Vishnu Sridhara on loan from the Brooklyn Museum (10). This image has more than its iconography in common with the Vishnu of the stone stele at Changu Narayan (VI). Yet it is more stark in its stiffness, more nude in the splendor of its golden radiance and the ornaments set with stones. The sacred thread is doubled and shortened. It passes under the waistbelt and the folded upper cloth whose ends, too, are shortened as are those of the dhoti.

Their pointed ends enliven the lower part of the image, supported on stiff, widespread legs. Here, once more, the powerful face is more Indian than Nepali. The horizontal ends of the band by which the crown is tied occur on images of a later date. The armlets of Vishnu are worn lower down than in the other images; clubs of this shape are also found on Vishnu images centuries later. On account of its stark power the image does not appear to be a later replica but seems to carry the type of the Vishnu image of Changu Narayan into the following centuries. While no definite date can be given to this figure, it is not as late as the eleventh century, when dated stone images completely different from this in form, like that of Surya (1065) at Thapahiti, Patan, are known (X).

Conservative in details of iconography and particularly of ornaments and drapery (6), and at the same time richly reflective of new currents from more than one Indian school, the sculptures between the eighth and eleventh century show a mingling of these currents within the overall Nepali form. The indigenous tradition which in the fifth century created the figure of the "king" from Mrigasthali, Pashupati (1), uses its own ferment and moves at its own pace while carrying along its native heritage, together with all that had been assimilated by absorbing contemporary Indian impressions (7). This process puts a distance between the sculptor and his work which owes more to his judgment or taste than to intuition. Suavity of form is his main concern.

VIII. Padmapani Avalokiteshvara.
Sigha Baha, Kathesimbhu, Katmandu, Nepal.
Ca. eighth century.

The depths of realization to which Indian sculpture gave form rested in India. Nepal has no Elephanta or Aurangabad of its own, but the shape of the female figure as developed in Aurangabad found its way to Nepal, and was given there a new body unlike, yet related to it. Besides, after the seventh century northern India, taking stock of past achievements, went on practising sculpture according to established and carefully followed rules. In the field of Buddhist art, the *Manjusrimulakalpa*, a text completed in the eighth century, speaks of Buddhism as declining and of the attempt being made to revive it through newly fashioned images. In Nepal this groping for new form and a new salvation is seen in the relief of the "nativity" of the Buddha, from Deo-Patan (11).

The tall figure of Maya Devi (11) surpasses the image of Avalokiteshvara of the Sigha Baha, Katmandu, by the assurance of its long, swinging contours. Her body carries the memories of the form of Gauri and of Yakshinis from Mathura. She reaches into the branches of the tree where a miracle of fruits and flowers is born from her hands. Their three-dimensional interlacement is the horizontal response on high to the crossing of legs and the garment's folded front piece. But tree and Maya Devi are only the frame for the Buddha who is born, the Lord of the World. Like a pillar, and supported by the lotus, the sturdy body of the child stands in the egg shape of his effulgence while the celestial streams flow to bathe the babe, and angels tilt their vessels brimming with lotuses, soft and moist in shape, in the eddy of the waters.

Seen against the Avalokiteshvara image of the Sigha Baha, a work of convention, the relief of Maya Devi, a work of purest creative Nepali invention, has mobilized Indian resources embedded in the tradition of the country. The face of Maya Devi and the form of the Buddha child seem related to types from Bihar of the eighth to ninth century.

Under the Licchavis and their successors (ca. 400—750 A. D.) the art of Nepal had felt the heartbeat of the Gupta tradition of Northern India, and took part in the culmination of creativeness which swayed India from the Deccan to Bihar in the seventh century. Reverberations of both these impacts continued into the eighth and ninth century.

At this time Hinduism no less than Buddhism produced newly fashioned images in Nepal. Vishnu had received the homage of the Nepali sculptor since the age of Manadeva, in compositions which served as models for centuries. Now the turn for Shiva images had come, and with it an array of representations of Uma-Maheshvara, the great Lord, together with Uma, his consort (IX). The elaboration of this image in Nepal follows one complex iconography in which contemporary Deccan elements such as those of Ellora are blended with central and northern Indian motifs preserved only in their later versions.[7] The center of these many-figured compositions is Shiva enthroned with Uma on Mount Kailasa. Two dated versions of this composition, one in 1012 and the other of the late twelfth century, differ as much from each other as both differ from images assignable to circa the eighth-ninth centuries (IX). These images are stone steles. To this group must be added a metal image of Uma-Maheshvara in the Baroda Museum (9).

The Eastern school of Indian art contributed nothing to this type of image, even when this school sent its illuminated manuscripts (cf. 78, 79) and probably also its painters to Nepal from about the year 1000. Far from accepting even single motifs from that school, once accomplished the compositional type of Uma-Maheshvara went through modifications which each sculptor brought about when he showed the god knowing himself in his togetherness with the goddess. To this knowledge Shiva gives exposition with his main right hand, while he embraces the goddess, to his left, with his main left hand. Sitting next to him, Uma rests her hand on his leg. She leans on the god. The torsion of her body, the cadence of her curves, vary with her mood and posture, which is one of ease, allowing the rhythms of listening and understanding to sway her entire shape, from her coiffure to the tips of her toes (IX, 9). In the Uma-Maheshvara images of the eastern school the goddess sits on the lap of the god. In this greater intimacy the freedom of response, its pause, and the organization of the figures together with their interspaces are absent.

During the rule of the Pala dynasty (750—1150) in Eastern India, bronze images were made in large numbers in Nalanda and Kurkihar in Bihar, and being easily portable (14) found their way to Nepal where their form at once became re-cast in the Nepali tradition (12, 13). In the early eleventh century the monastery of Vikramashila in the heart of the Pala empire had replaced Nalanda as a center of Buddhism. Among its brilliant teachers were three Nepalis. It was from there that Pandit Atisha, the founder of Tibetan Lamaism proceeded in 1040 to Tibet, by way of Nepal. In spite of renewed contacts and though the Pala style was closely followed, its Nepali versions are unmistakable in their suave line and expression. They extract from the ornate maturity of Sena sculptures a delicacy of feeling and an elegance not within reach of the East Indian bronzes. Although none of these Nepali bronzes is dated, they parallel the phases of Pala sculpture (12, 13, 15) and excel those of the subsequent Sena dynasty in Eastern India (16). The rich modeling of the Sena school is presented by the Newari sculptor as sensitively as are the ornaments. Its plasticity, however, has less tension than it had in the Sena school. The images appear not so much as direct embodiments steeped in glory but rather as if listening to the voice within which invests them with their radiance.

The homeland of the Sena rulers was in the Deccan. From the same region, the Kanarese country, came Nanyadeva, who conquered not only Tirhut (north Bihar) at the foot of the mountains of Nepal but also Nepal itself in 1094. Stone images of the Sena school, which had assimilated the ornateness of contemporary Kanarese sculpture, found their way into Nepal under Nanyadeva and his successors. By the end of the twelfth century, furthermore, the Muslim conquest of Bengal brought to Nepal refugee artists from Eastern India. It was then that the Eastern Indian art tradition was given a most subtle re-interpretation in Nepal (16).

Under the Thakuris and early Mallas (ca. 750 to 1480) the influence of the school of Eastern India was on the ascendancy from the tenth century, and reached its height in the thirteenth century. When A-ni-ko brought the art of Nepal to Tibet and China, local Nepali traits also attained maturity (18). Thereafter, delicacies of sentiment were carried, by an at times somewhat equivocal form (20, 23, 26), into the fifteenth century. By the sixteenth century the Mallas (1480—1768) had set up their power in three kingdoms. It is in this last phase of Newari creativeness that the Tantrik way of knowing the ultimately Real was given support by images of frenzied grandeur (29).

The stone sculptures after the tenth century do not keep pace in their quality with the bronzes. While metal images, both cast and repoussé, maintain their quality into the sixteenth century, and in less frequent instances into the nineteenth century, stone sculpture stagnates after absorbing the Sena impact. The creative artists of that phase were the workers in metal and wood.

No dated temple with wood carvings is known before 1394. With the small Bhairava shrine at Panoti (dated 514 N. S.) begins, to our knowledge, a prolific production which shows itself as strong in the eighteenth century as in the fourteenth. The singular phases of the wood carver's art (36, 62, 64, 72, 73) have not as yet been defined, nor have those of the carvers in rock crystal (63), ivory, and human bone (57), nor of workers in dry lacquer.

The Sena style remained the basis of the form of metal images in the thirteenth century although the modeling became more shallow and the contour more smoothly melodious (18). In the fourteenth century, with an increasingly summary modeling (19—22), the contour of the simplified volumes tightens with an arrested energy (23, 24). In the Newari response to the Sena style, the ornaments which formerly had enriched the effect of the sculptures became an essential and expressive part of the sculptural vision (16, 17).

Toward the end of the fourteenth century a renewed interest in modeling makes the surface of some images appear as if kneaded (25) or, where the intention is more descriptively suggestive, parts of the body, like the abdomen or thighs are made to appear resilient to the touch (26). The fourteenth and fifteenth centuries seem to abound in new creations, in different ramifications of an evolving style. Bodhisattva figures assignable to the earlier part of the fifteenth century (30, 31) are over-elongated in their slimness. As provocative as they are unearthly in their stance, they seem to sway while the figure, after having set foot in this world, halts. Toward the sixteenth

IX. Uma-Maheshvara.
Nagal Tol, Katmandu, Nepal.
Ca. eighth-ninth century.

century these slim, elongated figures swell with a new sap (38).

Meanwhile, in the third quarter of the fifteenth century, a more earthbound type, related to an image of Vasudhara dated A. D. 1467, had become established.[8] In these figures the fluency of the contour is interrupted and the torso sits on broad hips (32, 33, 37). Only rarely (34) is this type given the lyrical charm in which an image of Indra is steeped. In the fuller proportions which the figure is given toward the end of the fifteenth century, the work of the sixteenth century introduces itself (38). These two centuries correspond, not only in time but also in their sequence of artistic content, to the Renaissance in Italy.

From the end of the sixteenth century the form becomes dilated, charged with fierce or brooding emotion (55)—or desiccated by it (58). Images of the seventeenth century often have a dry correctness which rigorously preserves the sweet nobility of Newari tradion (56).

With an unprecedented elan, Tantrik images are given form (29, 85) from the mid-fifteenth to the eighteenth century. The *unio mystica* of the opposite principles in the sexual symbolism of Tantrik Buddhism is shown by the embrace of male and female images. The male image stands for the Buddha principle, which is compassionate throughout. The female image is Prajna or gnosis, the knowledge and symbol of the Absolute, *Shunya*, the Void. It is void of all contingencies, of all human limitations and egoity. By penetrating Prajna the Buddha expresses and confirms his Buddhahood. He is the means and Prajna is the end. Together they are the Realization of the Absolute.

For the sake of mankind, the Buddha principle in Tantrik Buddhism is made approachable to every man. In art, this principle has two types of shape, that of the Buddha image and that of the Yidam or tutelary divinity. The Buddha image symbolizes the state of Buddhahood, the Yidam its operation within the human heart. The many-limbed images of the Yidams in their dancing frenzy symbolize the moment of ecstasy, of being outside oneself, free from the self, the ego, with its manifold selfish interests and attachments. The many hands of the tutelary gods with their weapons and symbols cut and sever attachments. They liberate. It is a moment of rapture in which the Prajna participates and is being obtained. The ecstatic union of these images takes place in the mind of the Tantrik Buddhist.

The *sadhanas* or injunctions for the contemplation and making of images had been composed in India, centuries earlier. In the fifteenth to eighteenth centuries in Nepal, these ancient symbols became quickened not with new meaning but with new life, and the ability arose to project into the sanctioned forms an emotional immediacy amounting to frenzy, whether in the experience of the tremendous or the horrendous.

The symbols of sexual union in Indian art were experienced on many levels and served different meanings. In some of the Hindu sculptures of Konarak the carnal element was strong whereas in Khajuraho sentiment and savoir faire assuaged the form of these symbols.

In the eighteenth century the elan and power animating these images, although diminished, do not subside (68). An image of Durga, killing the buffalo demon (67; 1768) is still sustained by them. Where, however, the image-maker was called upon to create representations of divinity in its serene aspect, he accomplished showpieces whose spectacular beauty is distilled from more than a millennium of the unbroken tradition of Newari art (65, 66).

The metal images of "Lamaistic Buddhism" of the seventeenth and eighteenth centuries became familiar to the West in figures of average quality, produced in large quantities in Nepal, Tibet, and Mongolia. In China, preciosity was rationalized (70), and sweetened (71).

Paintings are known from Nepal only from the eleventh century. They followed the small illustrations of Buddhist scriptures on palm leaves and on their wooden book covers, which brought the Pala form of Eastern Indian painting to Nepal (74, 75, 77, 80). The earliest dated set of Nepali book covers (74; A. D. 1028) harmonious in its juxtaposition of images, circumscribes them with lines whose flux has a studied perfection, more meticulous and less immediate than those of Bengali workmanship. The flamboyant intricacies of scrollwork on thrones and mandorlas add an agitation controlled by their near-geometrical outline. When shown standing, the figures seem to float in their swaying stances; walking they glide and soar, forecasting the ambiguous stance of some latter day sculptures (30). Perennial traits of Nepali form are transmitted across the centuries. An illumination of the late sixteenth century may retain all the essentials of a composition created more than half a millennium earlier, yet be alive.[9]

All Nepali paintings whether on palm leaf, paper, wood or cloth are carried out in gouache. The metal images are cast in the lost wax process, or they are repoussé. More often than not they are gilded; if not, their faces may be painted with gold and the original polychromy of face and hair can sometimes still be seen (31). Sculpture and painting remain as closely related as they were in India, although modeling by color, shading and line is not as a rule the concern of the Newari painter. He is not always successful when he attempts it—as a book cover shows that is painted with the vivacity of folk art (75).[10] Only under the direct impact of the late Pala and Sena schools (78) do the highly modeled shapes of Nepali painting (80) relate to a tradition which stems from forms such as those in Ajanta. Modeling in color and shading, where it was retained, became residual and sporadic (77), although it persisted in certain horror-provoking images like that of Lhamo (Shri Devi) in a painting on cloth of the fifteenth century (86), intensifying the horror of the figure by making it almost tangible.

The meticulous finesse of miniature painting, with or without modeling, was replaced at the end of the fourteenth century by more schematic or else more sketchy, cursive outlines (81).[11] This technique was suited to a large demand for paintings by the "Yellow Church" founded in Tibet by Tson-kha-pa (1357—1419). The work of A-ni-ko and his eighty Nepali artists who had come to Tibet in 1260 was not forgotten by this time;[12] the Nor monastery in Southern Tibet, founded in 1429, invited many Nepali artists to paint its chapels. They and their pupils also painted on cloth hierarchs of the Sa Skya pa school, a large number of mandalas (87) and also patas (83). Nepali artists also worked in Western Tibet, in Guge.

Mandalas are visual supports of concentration and meditation, ritual aids on the way toward the Center of the cosmos and self. Cosmos and self coincide in the image of the central and main divinity of the mandala. This divinity resides, in principle, in an eight-petaled lotus filling a circle, within a square, enclosed by further concentric circles (87). The square is divided by diagonals into four triangles whose colors—white, yellow, red, and blue—represent the four directions. Entry and exit into the magically fortified square are marked in the middle of each side by a symbolic gate structure. Stations on the way are marked by small images of subsidiary divinities in their appointed places, in the eight directions of space within the square. As a rule, the rim of the surrounding circle teems with scenes. They illustrate the "eight cemeteries", the eightfold task of dying to the ego, to all worldly propensities of the self, in preparation for entering the citadel with its Center.

Outside the circle of the cemeteries and its border, aflame with the fire of gnosis which destroys ignorance, are painted auxiliary divinities, "perfect ones" (*siddha*), and hierarchs of the church. All these figures are drawn in miniature technique or in a spirited shorthand. Their colors are prescribed. Like their physiognomical types, movements and attributes, the colors serve as identifying cognizances. The individual artist's choice is restricted to the tonality of the total effect of the mandala, which he modifies by the density and variety of the scrollwork that covers the background areas wherever the mandala is without figures.

Mandala painting is an art applied to an instrument (*yantra*). It must be correctly made to fulfill its purpose, which is to serve as a chart or guide out of the chaos of the unconscious and the entanglements of the world. The execution of these instruments demands correctness and precision from the painter. Mandala painting strictly does not lend itself to the creative experience of the artist. Where it does, it approximates the form of a pata, a painting of images. Although this, too, is guided by prescription so that it conforms to the original conception and to its religious significance, it demands from the artist identification with his work. He who wants to paint an image, if he cannot be it, cannot paint it.[13] Over and above its prescribed iconography, a pata may be great art.

X. Surya. 1065 A. D.
Thapahiti, Patan,
Nepal.

45

Mandalas painted in Nepal (88, 92) are less rigorously controlled in their organization than those painted in the Tibetan monasteries (87). The central square houses the main divinity with the greater freedom of a pata and the scenes around the encompassing circle of the cemeteries —which may or may not be illustrated—are full of narrative in the earlier paintings, leaving little room for the images of the marginal divinities.

In addition to that of evocation of and identification with the divinity, the art of the pata served a magical purpose. By merely looking at a pata the faithful might achieve whatever he desired, be it illumination or health, wealth, and sons, a remission of his shortcomings, or an amelioration of his karma. Certain rites might be observed in preparing the cloth—or they could be omitted. All that was needed was faith and concentration on the evocative *mantra*, the magic formula uttered in front of the competently painted image. For this purpose the paintings described in the *Manjusrimulakalpa* showed not only the gods who were invoked but also their setting—the world ocean, mountains, clouds, a lotus lake—none of which figure in the paintings on cloth in Nepali style found at Tun Huang in westernmost China, nor in those from Nepal and Tibet from about 1400 A. D. The ground of these last is an opaque color surface, or may be vibrant with all-over patterns of closely traced scrollwork in a somewhat lighter tone of the color of the ground.

The paintings, whether mandala or pata, are on coarse cotton when from Nepal and on fine cotton cloth when painted in Tibet, the ground being sized with a mixture of chalk and glue; the colors, being likewise mixed with glue, become one with the ground. The finished painting is varnished with the white of a duck's egg mixed with water.

As in sculpture, so also in painting, the period from the later part of the fourteenth to the late sixteenth century provided (particularly in its earlier part) works of an intimate nobility and contained power (84). The sixteenth century presented the sacred themes with assurance although, toward the end, with a heavier hand and an admixture of folk art elements (89; 1570).

The large figure of the main deity in its aureole (*prabhamandala*) occupies the center of the painting. Particulary in the earlier paintings (82, dated 1436; 84) it would seem that some work of sculpture, complete with its back-stele for aureole (VI, VII) must have ruled over the vision of the painter. He translated it into a picture, giving the ground not only color but also, as a rule, a cover of scrollwork as dense as moss. Deep Indian reds, equally deep and mellow blues and greens, enlivened by golden yellow and white, are the choice in Nepal (88) whereas the palette of the Nepali school in Tibet is brighter, less restricted and at the same time colder (83). Furthermore, Chinese motifs of textile origin add their lightness to some of the paintings of the Nepali school in Tibet.

The composition of the patas is symmetrically ordered following the structure of the throne of the central image (82, 83). Border zones accommodate further images, groups or scenes, each in a compartment of its own (84). It is as if these small scale illuminations might have been taken from the pages of a volume containing all the images and scenes which formed the repertory of this art—and been placed in the sequence required by each pata. In addition, there is an array of portraits of the donor and his family in one or more compartments at the bottom of the pata, showing royalty or citizens in the costume becoming to their status and following the fashion of the day (82, 84, 88).

In some patas the vision of deity is overwhelming. It pushes aside the multiplicity of small scenes (85, 86). In the heat of the apparition of Mahakala (86) they coalesce in a turmoil of shapes. And yet, even this visual precipitation of destructive-creative energy is ordered, following freely the rigorous scheme of the mandala, its eight cemeteries being massed in the four directions. Whereas the painter of this pata is unknown, the name of the master (mahapatra) of the other pata (85) is given in its inscription together with that of the donor, King Ratnamalla, in the year 1467. The Malla kings were great patrons of art. They gave Nepal its palaces and temples. Without them Nepal would not be what it is. Their towers are as much a part of Nepal as are the snow-clad mountains. The name of King Ratnamalla is also given on a pata of Vajradhara, of the year 1488.[14] Ratnamalla, himself a Hindu, in his endeavor not only to further the already extant

assimilation of Buddhism and Hinduism but to merge the one in the other, recognized in the Adi-Buddha a form of Devi, the Hindu Great Goddess. Similarly, he associated his name with the installation of Buddhist gods.

It was in his long reign of over seventy years that the first Muslims came to Nepal. While their arrival might have contributed to the religious policy of the King, it had no political consequence. Its effect is barely noticeable in the illustrations of a paper manuscript of the *Hitopadesha* of the year 1594 (90, A-C). This book of "profitable instruction", a compilation from the *Pancatantra*, imparts its worldly wisdom by means of fables. These spread over the world, were translated into sixty languages, and are here illustrated with sophisticated vigor and Nepali charm.

A certain recrudescence of folk art in a pata of the later part of the sixteenth century (89; 1570) does not indicate a decline in the art of the pata. Deeply rooted in tradition, paintings full of zest and delicacy (95) were created in the seventeenth-eighteenth centuries (98).

By that time, Rajasthani as well as Chinese-Tibetan elements had been integrated into Nepali painting, as revealed in a long scroll (96; 1635). The seventeenth-eighteenth centuries recaptured the splendors of the fifteenth century and lent them a resilient and elegant line (98). In Tibet, in the seventeenth century, the Tibetan mode of painting was consolidated as a style of its own. Whereas Nepali masters were the teachers of

Tibetan artists in the fourteenth and fifteenth centuries, the Tibetan style had found its way to Nepal by the middle of the seventeenth century, as two paintings dated 1662 in the Indian Museum, Calcutta, go to prove.[15] The Nepali style of the pata however remained vital into the mid eighteenth century (102; 1755). Its images are set against a flat, opaque ground, even though leafy tendrils appearing on it are arranged in a new perspective. The Nepali pata of the traditional type remains a painted iconostasis. On the other hand, a Tibetan tanka (104) of that phase suspends its images as part of an invisible curtain across a landscape fantasy of Chinese origin. The Nepali pata of the traditional type resisted the intrusion of "nature" and the illusion of three dimensional space. Even in the nineteenth century it retained its power over the many heterogeneous elements which had come to crowd the surface of a pata of 1862 (in the Bharat Kala Bhavan, Banaras).

This spatial illusion, however, did enter Nepali painting. It came from India together with the Rajasthani style of the seventeenth century. Rajasthani painting had absorbed, through an assimilation of Muslim painting and particularly of Mogul painting, some of the perspectives of Persian as also of Western Renaissance painting. The impact of Rajasthani painting proved irresistible, particularly to the Nepali painters of the long narrative scrolls.

These narrative scrolls are among the most ancient modes of pictorial composition in India. Transferred to the walls they had formed long friezes in the cave temples of Ajanta at the beginning of the Christian era; translated into relief they adorned the crossbars of the gates at Sanchi.

In the early seventeenth century, as the scroll dated 1635 shows (96), the composition representing twelve holy places of pilgrimage in Nepal consisted of oblong compartments of contrasting, opaque, colors in free, rhythmical sequence, with an occasional horizon line in some of them. This sixteenth to seventeenth century Rajasthani mode was superseded; only the format was retained in the lively narrative of the scrolls in the Rajasthani-Nepali style painted after the early eighteenth century (99, 101, 103). A long narrative scroll in the British Museum dated 1705, illustrating the story of Lord Buddha, shows not only Western perspective, such as seventeenth century Indian Rajasthani painting had brought to Nepal, but also Indian and Muslim figures and their costumes. This new style also appears in wall paintings in the palace at Bhatgaon. It invades some of the patas which, at this time, also incorporated the landscape of the Tibetan tankas, while other patas continued to be painted in the traditional Nepali style. The new style, its Rajasthani elements supplemented at times by Chinoiseries transmitted through Tibetan painting, also enters early eighteenth century Buddhist book illustrations (100 B). There the high horizons are overlapped by the mountains of Nepal.

More than a hundred years later, in the middle of the nineteenth century, all these elements are combined in zestful spontaneity in some large scale album leaves (105, 106). Deeds of valor from ancient Indian tales are re-enacted in a landscape of mountain crags as only a Nepali artist of the nineteenth century could paint them.

To this day Nepal has a living myth. It is enacted throughout the year in the succession of seasonal rites and festivals. No living art supports them any longer. It has withdrawn and may be hiding in the golden casket guarded by the Fire Serpent, if the lake which was aflame has not become a fallow field.

NOTES

1. Daniel Wright, *History of Nepal* (Cambridge, 1877), p. 118; S. Levi, *Le Népal* (Paris, 1905), Vol. I, p. 385, Vol. II, p. 96; D. L. Regmi, *Ancient Nepal* (Calcutta, 1960), p. 78. The Shaka, and not the "Licchavi" era, however determines the date of Manadeva, see D. G. Sirkar, *Select Inscriptions bearing on Indian History and Civilization* (Calcutta, 1942), p. 366, note 1.
The chronology of the rule of Vrishadeva is not the same in the local chronicles. The decisive event, moreover, according to the chronicle used by S. Levi, took place when Vrishadeva was miraculously resurrected. Miracle and legend are interwoven with history. Vrishadeva's reign seems to coincide with that of the Indian emperor Samudragupta.

2. This does not preclude their existence. The Buddhist images, however, which have been assigned to the fifth and sixth centuries because of their style, belong to the eighth century (see "Arte del Nepal" by H. Goetz, *Le Civiltà dell'Oriente* (Roma, 1962), and "Early Indian Sculpture from Nepal," *Artibus Asiae*, XV (1955), p. 67 f.

3. Coins of Kadphises I and II; cf. E. H. Walsh, *Journal of the Royal Asiatic Society*, 1908, p. 681; V. Smith, *Catalogue of Indian Coins* (Oxford), p. 179.

4. The photograph, taken many years ago by a Nepali photographer, does not show the entire sculpture, which is at present inaccessible.

5. Dying King Narendradeva bequeathed his crown, with a copy of the *Prajnaparamita* (scripture) to his two daughters (Levi, *op. cit.*, Vol. II, p. 164). This was in 780 A. D. The style of the stele would agree with this date and it is possible that the two royal ladies represent the daughters of King Narendradeva.

6. In an article to be published in *Artibus Asiae* on "A Pre-Pala Sculpture and Its Significance for the International Bodhisattva Style in Asia," John D. LaPlante

discusses this image at length. His conclusions about the date of the image—the seventh century—agree with those arrived at by the writer. Mr. LaPlante, however, would assign the image—identified by him as Ghantapani—to Northern India rather than Nepal. The object held in the right hand is not a bell (*ghanta*). The somewhat later image of Bodhisattva Vajrapani of the *Licchavi Caitya*, Nag Baha, Patan, holds in his right hand another kind of rounded shape. The right hand of both these images seems to hold a fruit. According to the *Manjusrimulakalpa* (M. Lalou, *Iconographie des Etoffes Peintes dans le Manjusrimulakalpa* [Paris, 1930] p. 14) Bodhisattvas hold a fruit (*phala*) in their hands. This vague specification applies to the two images. In other sculptures the right hand of Vajrapani is empty.

7. Stella Kramrisch, *The Hindu Temple* (Calcutta, 1946), Vol. II, Pl. LV, the flying figure. This illustration shows a rudimentary form of the flying figure. It is represented in full shape in many other Nepali Uma-Maheshvara images of the same period as the one illustrated here.

8. Between a stone image of Mahagauri in Deo-Patan of the year 1205, and a metal image of Vasudhara of the year 1467 (the latter reproduced in *Oriental Art*, 1959, p. 91, Fig. 2), a few dated images are said to exist, but could not be traced.

9. One only has to compare the scene of Buddha's nativity and his taking possession of the world, shown on these book covers and in a manuscript of *Prajnaparamita* dated A. D. 1570, in the Asutosh Museum of Indian Art, University of Calcutta. The more cursive and less careful drawing of the page in the Asutosh Museum is a sign of its later date. Moreover the crowded group of Maya Devi and her sister in the Asutosh Museum page lacks the sophistication of composition on the book cover.

10. Cf. also the earliest extant Nepali palm leaf manuscript, dated A. D. 1015 (Cambridge, Ms. Add. 1643); A. Foucher, *Etude sur l'Iconographie Bouddhique de l'Inde* (Paris, 1900), Pls I. 3, 4; II. 4; VI. 3, etc.

11. Manuscripts of this type are in the Bir Library, Katmandu; a *Jayaksharasamhita* and a *Nityahnikatilaka*, both dated 1395, the latter reproduced, Kramrisch, "Nepalese Painting," *Journal of the Indian Society of Oriental Art*, I (Calcutta, 1933), p. 147.

12. A pata (G. Tucci, *Tibetan Painted Scrolls* [Rome, 1949], Pl. B; and Benjamin Rowland, Jr., *The Evolution of the Buddha Image*, The Asia Society [New York, 1963], Pl. 26) has been assigned to the fourteenth century. Another pata of the same series is in the Bharat Kala Bhavan, Banaras Hindu University. A third painting of this style is in a private collection, New York. Two very large patas, one in a private collection, New York, the other in London, could also be assigned to this phase.

13. "Dante sums up the whole matter from the medieval point of view when he says 'He who would paint a figure, if he cannot be it, cannot paint it.' (Convivio, Canzone III, 53—54) or as he otherwise expressed it 'No painter can portray any figure, if he have not first of all made himself such as the figure ought to be' (ib. IV, 10, 106, p. 309 of the Oxford Text)." Ananda K. Coomaraswamy, "The Intellectual Operation in Indian Art," *Journal of the Indian Society of Oriental Art*, June 1935, p. 9.

14. The composition of this painting is similar to though more sensitive than that of Lokeshvara, dated 1570 (91). Cf. Odette Monod-Bruhl, "Une Peinture Nepalaise du Musée Guimet," *Arts Asiatiques*, VI (1959), color plate facing p. 297.

15. *Archaeological Survey of India, Annual Report*, 1923—24, p. 103.

65. White Tara.   Eighteenth century.   H : 22$^1/_2$".

PLATES

SCULPTURE

54

2. Devi (Gauri or Tara). Seventh century. H: 28″.

◀ 1. Statue of a King (?).
Early fifth century. H: 16½″.

3. Tara (or Gauri).   Seventh century.   H: 8″.

4. Devi.   Seventh century.   H: 6$\frac{1}{8}$″.   ▶

5. Vajrapani.   Seventh century.   H: 10¹/₄″.

6. **Buddha Maitreya. Seventh–eighth century.   H: 6⁷/₁₆".**

9. Uma–Maheshvara. Eighth–ninth century. H: 4³⁄₄″.

◄ 7. Nimbate figure and attendant. Late eighth century. H: 5¹⁄₂″.

11. Nativity of the Buddha.   Ninth century.   H : 33″.

◄ 14. Vishnu in Lotus-mandala.
   Eastern Indian School.   Early twelfth century.   H: 5″.

10. Vishnu.   Ninth century (?).   H: 9¹¹/₁₆″.

18. Indra. Thirteenth century. H : 10″. ▶

◀ 16. Indra. Ca. 1200. H : 15⁷/₈″.

66

19. Avalokiteshvara. Fourteenth century (?). H: 24³/₄″.

21. Prajnaparamita. Fourteenth century. H: 9″.

15. Vasudhara. Early twelfth century. H: 6¼″.

26. Tara.   End fourteenth century.   H: 36″.

28. Nagas. Ca. seventeenth century. H: ca. 2¼″.

23. Vasudhara.   Fourteenth century.   H : 5″.

35. Arapacana Manjusri.   Fifteenth century.   H: 3³/₄″.

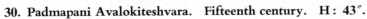

30. Padmapani Avalokiteshvara.   Fifteenth century.   H: 43″.

◄ **29. Navatmaka Heruka.   Seventeenth-eighteenth century.   H: 9¹/₂″.**

33. Indra. Fifteenth century. H: 10″.

38. Vajrapani. **Late fifteenth century.** H : 8″.

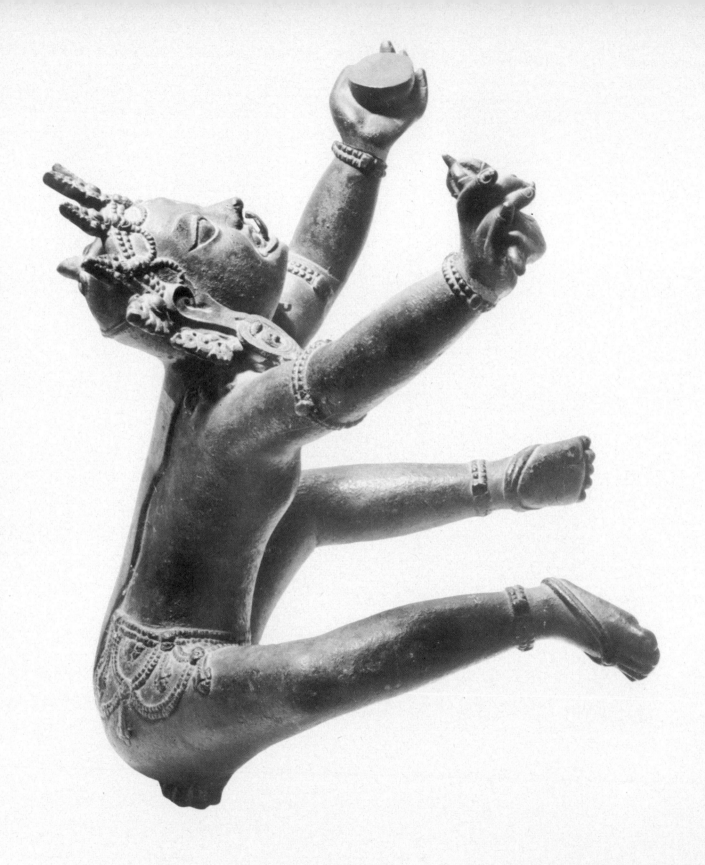

40. **Consort of Vrisha-Samvara.**
    Ca. late fifteenth century.   H : 14$\frac{1}{2}$".

44. Bull. Fifteenth–sixteenth century. H: 2³/₄″.

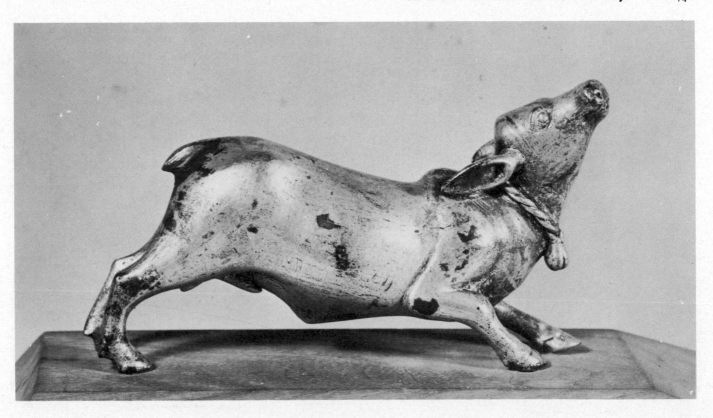

41. Krishna. Fifteenth–sixteenth century. H : 6³/₄″.

46. Vasudhara. Beginning sixteenth century. H: 6³/₈″.

48. Prabha-mandala. Sixteenth century. H: 12¹/₈″.

82

54. Udiyana Kurukulla. Sixteenth century.   H : 7¹⁄₄″.

**47. Ucchushma Jambhala and Vasudhara.
Early sixteenth century.   H : 1⁵⁄₈″.**

50. Tara.   Sixteenth century.   H : 5″.

51. Lokeshvara. Sixteenth century. H: 9⅛″.

52. Akshobhya. Sixteenth century. H: 7¼″.

55. Indra.   Sixteenth–seventeenth century.   H: 11″.

57. Plaque from a ritual apron. Sixteenth–seventeenth century. H: $6^5/_8''$; W: $1^3/_4''$.

53. Vasya-Vajravarahi. Sixteenth century (?). H: 25″.

60. Arapacana Manjusri. Mongolia (?).
Seventeenth century. H: 5″.

61. Bhairava (?). Tibet.
Seventeenth century. H: 4″.

62. Padmapani.   Seventeenth century.   H : 6″.

63. Buddha Sheltered by a Serpent.   Seventeenth century.   H : 5$^1/_8$″.

64. Tara.   Seventeenth–eighteenth century.   H : 12$^1/_2$″.

◄ **66. White Tara.   Eighteenth century.   H : 22″.**

67. Durga Killing the Buffalo Demon.   Dated 1768.   H : 12".

68. Samvara.   Eighteenth century.   H : 14".

71. Bodhisattva. China (Peking). Eighteenth century. H: 18″.

90 A—C. Hitopadesha.   Dated 1594.   Three pages : each $2\,^5/_8''\times 8\,^3/_4''$.

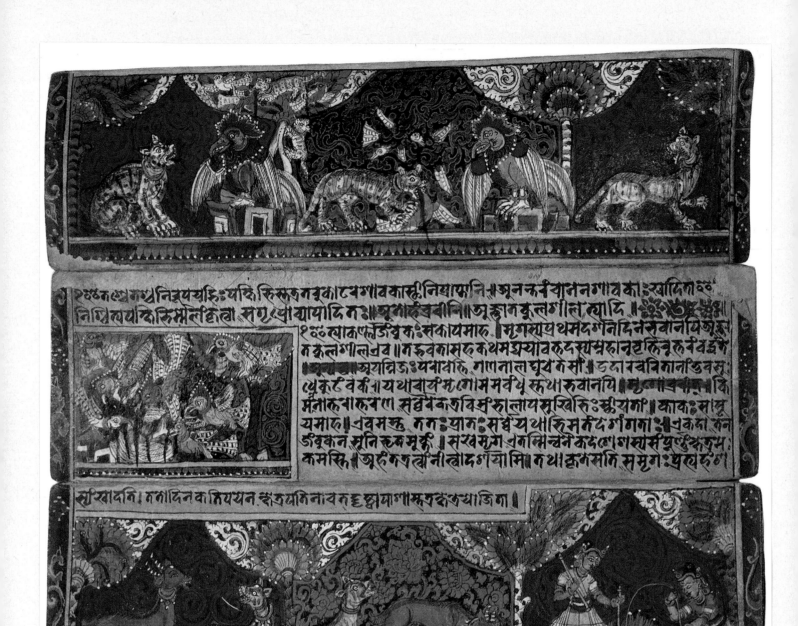

PLATES

PAINTINGS AND MANUSCRIPTS

80. Shivadharma.   Painted book cover.   Thirteenth century. $3\frac{7}{8}'' \times 21\frac{3}{16}''$.

78. Leaf from a Gunakarandavyuha (?). Eastern Indian School. Twelfth century. $2'' \times 21^{5}/_{8}''$ (detail).

81. Zodiacal signs and divinities.   End of fourteenth or early fifteenth century. $4^3/_8'' \times 10^5/_8''$.

74. A book cover of an Ashtasahasrika Prajnaparamita (Book of the Perfection of Wisdom). Dated 1028. $2^1/_2'' \times 17^1/_4''$ (detail).

75. A book cover of an Ashtasahasrika Prajnaparamita. Ca. mid-eleventh century. $2^{1}/_{8}'' \times 22''$.

77. A book cover from an Ashtasahasrika Prajnaparamita. Dated 1110 A.D. $2^{1}/_{2}'' \times 22^{7}/_{16}''$ (detail).

◄ 82. Amoghapasha Avalokiteshvara.
Pata.   Dated 1436.   22$^1/_2$″ × 17$^1/_2$″.

85. Traylokyavijaya (?) Pata.   Dated 1467.   42$^3/_4$″ × 27$^1/_2$″.

88. Vasudhara Mandala.   Ca. 1504.   37$^1/_2$″ × 26″.

83. **Adi-Buddha Vajradhara. Pata. Nepali School of Nor Monastery, S. Tibet. First half fifteenth century.** $33^{7}/_{8}'' \times 31^{1}/_{4}''$.

86. Mahakala, Protector of the Tent. Pata. Nepal School in Tibet. Fifteenth century. $38^{1}/_{4}'' \times 26^{1}/_{4}''$ (detail).

89. Lokeshvara (Sukhavati?) and Tara.   Pata.   Dated 1570. $22^3/_4'' \times 18''$.

91. Siddhas, Hierarchs, etc.   Pata.   Sixteenth century.   22$^{11}/_{16}$" × 19$^{3}/_{4}$".

92.
Vasudhara
Mandala.
Pata.
Sixteenth century.
45³/₈″ × 35¹/₄.

93. ▶
Stupa. Pata.
Late sixteenth
century.
37³/₄″ × 18³/₄″.

96. Tirtha Mahatmya. Dated 1635. $15^3/_8'' \times 51^1/_4''$.

95. Chakrasamvara.
Pata.
Sixteenth-seventeenth
century.
$57^{1}/_{2}'' \times 32^{3}/_{16}''$.

97. Pata of
Dharmadhatu
Vagishvara.
Dated 1664.
59³/₄″ ×31″.

98. Vajravarahi Mandala. Seventeenth–eighteenth century. 41$\frac{1}{2}''$ × 28$\frac{1}{8}''$.

100b. Leaf from an Ashtasahasrika Prajnaparamita (detail).

100a. Book cover from an Ashtasahasrika Prajnaparamita. Early eighteenth century. $4\frac{1}{2}'' \times 18''$.

101. Vishnu Pata.
Ca. 1810. 20″ × 202″ (details).

102. Assemblage of images.
Pata. Dated 1775. 29¹/₈″ × 22″. ▶

103. The Story of Banasura. Later part of eighteenth century (?). $29^{1}/_{2}'' \times 141^{3}/_{4}''$.

104. Navatmaka Heruka. Tanka. Tibet. Eighteenth century. $17^1/_2'' \times 12^1/_2''$.

105, 106. Illustrations from a Bhagavata Purana. Middle of nineteenth century. $14^{1}/_{8}'' \times 20^{1}/_{2}''$

88. Vasudhara Mandala.   Ca. 1504. $37^1/_2'' \times 26''$ (detail).

The dates given the works of art are meant to suggest a relative chronology. Very few of the works are inscribed with dates, and, in many instances, lack of comparable objects precludes any but a tentative dating. All works, unless otherwise designated, are of Nepali origin.

Although Nepali metal sculptures are ordinarily referred to as "bronzes" they are actually largely composed of copper. Some cataloguers quite reasonably designate them as copper images. In Nepal and India, however, these metal figures are known as made of *Ashta-dhatu* (eight "elements" or metals). The eight metals include gold and silver.

3

4

1. **Statue of a King (?). Early fifth century. Dark limestone. H : 16 1/2 ".
Gorakshanath Monastery, Mrigasthali, Pashupati, Nepal.**

The disciplined power of this figure, one of the earliest sculptures from Nepal as yet known, has been given a consistently Nepali form. Although nimbate, the figure is without attributes or gestures that would identify it as a divinity.

2. **Devi (Gauri or Tara). Seventh century. Dark limestone. H : 28 ".
Gift of His Majesty King Mahendra Bir Bikram Shah Deva to Stella Kramrisch.**

The smooth, rounded volumes of the body are set off by the mass of pleated drapery and by the scrollwork which is merged with it (V) and enriches the different levels of this stele from Deo-Patan, Nepal. Right arm and head are missing.

3. **Tara (or Gauri). Seventh century. Bronze. H : 8 ".
Lent anonymously.**

The high percentage of gold in this bronze has prevented patination and gives a subdued golden glow to the surface, inlaid with gold and silver.

4. **Devi. Seventh century. Copper. H : 6 1/8 ".
George P. Bickford Collection, Cleveland, Ohio.**

The goddess has raised her left hand before her breast in *kataka hasta*, the pendant right hand holds a fruit (?) with the gesture of giving a boon.

5. **Vajrapani. Seventh century. Gilt copper. H : 10 1/4 ".
Stanford University Museum, Stanford, California. Gift of Mrs. E. H. Heller.**

The Bodhisattva "Thunderbolt in Hand" (*Vajra-pani*) holds this symbol in his left hand and seems to have a fruit in his raised right hand. Standing on a double lotus pedestal, his sturdy figure gives the assurance that he discharges the Bodhisattva vow of renouncing his own salvation, while on the verge of attaining it, in order to work for the liberation of all living beings. Published: John D. LaPlante, "A Pre-Pala Sculpture and its Significance for the International Bodhisattva Style in Asia," *Artibus Asiae*, 1964 (in the press).

6. **Buddha Maitreya. Seventh-eighth century. Copper. H : 6 7/16 ".
The Cleveland Museum of Art, Cleveland, Ohio. Gift of Mr. and Mrs. Ralph King.**

Seated in *paryankasana*, with knees apart and feet firmly placed on the ground, the Future Buddha holds his hands in an eloquent gesture. His robe, massed in folds on either side of the figure—similar to those of the Buddha images of the *Licchavi Chaitya*, Dhvaka Baha, Katmandu—provides a transition between the figure and the broad seat. The lotus scroll decoration of the footstool is of a type similar to that of (VI) and (2). Traces of gold leaf remain.

7

7. **Nimbate figure and attendant. Late eighth century. Copper. H : 5¹/₂″.**
Collection of Nasli and Alice Heeramaneck, New York City.

Wearing only few and simple ornaments and no sacred thread, the bare body cinctured by a waistband, the short, striped loincloth held by a belt, the upper garment folded around the hips and knotted on the right, this tall, noble figure is crowned by a high, plain mitre having a raised circle in the center. A simple, pointed, oval halo enhances its importance. In his lower right hand he holds, with *hamsasya mudra*, expressing benediction, a small round object, possibly a fruit. The right hand rests on the head of an attendant whose sturdy, small shape accentuates the height of the nimbate figure. The arms of the attendant are crossed in front of the chest conveying disciplined submissiveness (*vinaya hasta*). The stance of the main figure is a modification of the pose of a "world-ruler" (*cakravartin*), standing straight, with legs apart, one arm akimbo.

8. **Garuda. Seventh-ninth century. Bronze. H : 4¹/₄″.**
Collection of Nasli and Alice Heeramaneck, New York City.

Garuda, the sun-bird, kneels holding a serpent, with folded hands, on a square, double pedestal impressed with the rectilinear design of rocks. This rock pedestal, rather than the lotus pedestal, belongs to the figure of Garuda in early Nepali Sculpture. His stylized wing-cape and the array of his locks enhance the forward tilt of his sturdy body, as if he had just alighted. Serpents are wreathed around his neck and arms. Except for the wings, the shape of the diademmed sun-bird is altogether human.

9. **Uma-Maheshvara. Eighth-ninth century. Bronze. H : 4³/₄″.**
Baroda Museum and Picture Gallery, Baroda, India.

While the image conforms with the style of stone carvings assignable to the eighth-ninth century, it differs from bronze images of later periods in the soft fullness of the modeled face, contrasting with the sharp delineation and pointedness of the features and their linear exaggerations. The modeling still owes something to Gupta tradition. However, it is not derived from the Vishnu from Nalanda, the earliest dated metal image of the Pala school (fourth decade of the ninth century), with which it is nearly coeval. (Cf. R. D. Banerji, *Eastern Indian School of Mediaeval Sculpture*, Delhi, 1933, Pl. Ib.) Published: P. H. Pott, "The Tibetan and Nepalese Collections of the Baroda Museum," *Bulletin of the Baroda Museum and Picture Gallery*, IX, 1953, p. 1—7.

8

12

12

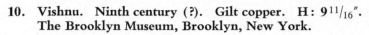

**10. Vishnu. Ninth century (?). Gilt copper. H: 9 11/16″.
The Brooklyn Museum, Brooklyn, New York.**

This gilded image is even more closely related to the images of Vishnu on a *Licchavi Chaitya* in the Taleju Temple, Katmandu, than to the stele in Changu Narayan (VI). Two bosses in the main right hand replace the lotus of Vishnu. The club has been damaged and is now bent. Published: George J. Lee, "Two Nepalese Sculptures," *Brooklyn Museum Bulletin* IX, 1958, p. 67, Fig. 2.

**11. Nativity of the Buddha. Ninth century. Black limestone. H: 33″.
Sundhara Fountain, Deo-Patan, Nepal.**

The birth of the Buddha from the right side of his mother, Maya, is shown in this relief by the traditional pose of Maya Devi under the Ashoka tree. Three separate elements, the woman-and-tree motif, the clouds and flying Devaputras, and thirdly the Buddha child with lotus pedestal and aureole, here coalesce.

**12. Bodhisattva Padmapani. Ninth-tenth century. Gilt copper. H: 7″.
Mrs. Edgar J. Stone, Toronto, Ontario, Canada.**

The awkward stance and the overlarge hand with the boon-giving gesture impart an impetuous immediacy to the figurine which is also expressed by the lotus flower, its petals opening as it were before our eyes. The face, of Indian type, is equivocal and alluring in its expression. The stance is a variant of that of the Padmapani, Boston Museum of Fine Arts; see A. K. Coomaraswamy, *History of Indian and Indonesian Art*, 1927, New York, Pl. XCV, Fig. 176.

**13. Tara. Early tenth century. Copper. H: 5″.
Collection of Nasli and Alice Heeramaneck, New York City.**

Similar in the ambivalent expression of the face to the Padmapani (12), this well-balanced figurine parallels the style of Pala sculptures of Eastern India of the early tenth century.

**14. Vishnu in Lotus-mandala. Eastern Indian School. Early twelfth century. Bronze. H: 5″.
The Ashmolean Museum, Oxford, England.**

Vishnu, enthroned on the seed pod of a lotus, is surrounded by eight (?) of his incarnations (avatars) or "descents" to the earth. They include the Man-lion, the Boar, and Rama from the standard ten incarnations and also others, like Dattatreya, which are innumerable. Each of these diminutive images is seated on a lotus pedestal, inside a petal of the lotus-mandala. The petals are hinged to the base around the seed pod and are movable; when the petals are closed, the divinities are concealed. The low, circular stand of this mandala of manifestation and withdrawal has lotus petals on its main molding. Nepali numbers appear on base and petals. Similar, more ornate and less architectonically composed lotus-mandalas reveal in the center of their seven petals the Tantrik Buddhist goddess Vajratara. (Cf. R. D. Banerji, op .cit., Pl. LXXII; H. Goetz, *Baroda Museum and Picture Gallery Handbook*, Baroda 1952, Pl. XXIX.)

15. Vasudhara. Early twelfth century. Gilt Bronze. H: 6¹/₄″. Collection of Nasli and Alice Heeramaneck, New York City.

Vasudhara, the Giver of Wealth, is here represented as a young girl according to the *sadhana*, the formula which prescribes how a divinity should be conceived. Closely related to late Pala sculpture, the image, which is inlaid with gems, is remarkable for the warmth of expression and sensitive modeling. The ears of corn, attribute of the goddess, are missing.

13

16. Indra. Ca. 1200. Gilt copper. H: 15⁷/₈″. Lent anonymously.

Seated at ease in *sukhasana*, the right hand raised before the chest in the gesture of exposition (*vyakhyana mudra*), the left supporting the upright body which is but slightly flexed at the hips, this ornate image of Indra, king of the gods, whose third eye is always shown horizontally on his forehead, differs from all other images of this god by its three-peaked crown and sacred thread tucked under the knotted waistband. The modeling of the image is close to that of Sena sculpture which it excels in delicacy and immanent power. Encrusted with spinel rubies, rock crystal and turquoise. Published: *Bulletin of the Philadelphia Museum of Art*, LV, 1960, p. 26.

17. Khadiravani Tara. Thirteenth century. Gilt copper. H: 9¹/₂″. Philadelphia Museum of Art, Philadelphia, Pennsylvania.

This image of the Green Tara with the blue lotus (*nilotpala*) on her left, and the *padma*-lotus on her right, seated in a posture of ease (*lalitasana*), the over-large right hand in *varada mudra*, shows by the equivocal expression of her face that, according to the *sadhana*, "she is full of jealousy." The pedestal is missing.

17

18. Indra. Thirteenth century. Bronze. H: 10″. Seattle Art Museum, Seattle, Washington. Eugene Fuller Memorial Collection.

The image of Indra is dear to the myth and art of Nepal. The best that the Newari sculptor had to give often went into the making of images of Indra. In a pensive and relaxed mood, Indra's right arm rests on his right knee; the drooping hand reinforces the elegant, linear movement which gives melodious significance to every limb and ornament. Although the

22

jewelry is simpler than that of Indra as shown in pl. 16, it plays a very prominent part in the composition, setting off the modeling, which here is more abstract. The broad *kirita mukuta* or crown of Indra, a high shield in front of the piled up hair, is fastened around the head, as are all the crowns, by bands whose ends form rosettes or pleated clusters above the ears. Here they accentuate the arc of the forehead, whereas the earrings link the angles of movement of head and body. Published: H. Zimmer, *The Art of Indian Asia*, New York, 1955, Pls. 598, 599.

19. Avalokiteshvara. Fourteenth century (?). Gilt copper. H : 24³/₄″. Cincinnati Art Museum, Cincinnati, Ohio.

The schematization and residual modeling of this image represent the aftermath of moments full of plastic vitality. The somewhat stilted movement, the arrested mobility of the line are characteristically Nepali. The ornaments of this image, which are almost without incrustation, lie as thick as fur on body and crown.

20. Avalokiteshvara. Ca. fourteenth century. Copper gilt. H : 36″. Golden Monastery (Hiranyavarna Mahavihara), Patan, Nepal.

The image, seated in *virasana*, is heavy in treatment. The end of the upper garment on the left shoulder is derived from a Pala motif. The lateral peaks of the crown are bent inward, pointing to the central crest which carries an image of Buddha Amitabha, the spiritual father of Bodhisattva Avalokiteshvara. The image is not encrusted with gems.

21. Prajnaparamita. Fourteenth century. Gilt bronze. H : 9″. Mr. Christmas Humphreys, London, England.

Prajnaparamita, goddess of "Transcendental Wisdom," holds in her raised left hand the *Book of Transcendental Wisdom*, the Scripture of Mahayana Buddhism, of which she is the embodiment. The two main hands have the gesture of teaching (*dharmacakra mudra*). The distended outer contour of the raised forearm was for centuries a mannerism of Newari sculpture (VI). In this image, "Transcendental Wisdom" in the fulness of her shape, appears as the Great Mother. Published: D. Barrett, "The Buddhist Art of Tibet and Nepal," *Oriental Art*, III (1957), p. 92, Fig. 6.

24

22. Janguli (?). Ca. fourteenth century. Gilt copper. H : 2³/₈″. Dr. and Mrs. Samuel Eilenberg, New York City.

The thunderbolt (*vajra*) in one of the right hands and the threatening gesture (*tarjani*) of one of the left hands are the only distinguishing signs which remain for an identification of this goddess with three faces and six arms.

23. Vasudhara. Fourteenth century. Copper gilt. H: 5˝.
Nelson Gallery—Atkins Museum, Kansas City, Missouri. Nelson Fund.

Although lacking the rich plasticity of an earlier image of the goddess (15), this figure is balanced in its structure and clear contour. The attributes in her left hands (book, ears of corn, overflowing vase) are as carefully placed as the folded end of her loincloth. Her main right hand with one finger pointing downward, does not, as prescribed, show the gesture of giving (*varada mudra*). As in the earlier image, the goddess wears her hair in two lateral buns, an ancient fashion known in India from sixth century.

24. Indra. Fourteenth century. Gilt bronze. H: 5³/₄˝.
Mr. J. J. Klejman, New York City.

As in the image of Padmapani, a lotus ascends from Indra's left hand to his shoulder where its open flower carries his weapon, the thunderbolt (*vajra*). The fingers of the drooping right hand, resting on the knee, show the *vyakhyana mudra*. The head slightly bent forward, and the body pulled back, make this spontaneous movement the focus of the composition. Its zest is expressed in a modeling which has eliminated the detailed "naturalism" of the Sena school. Simplified and hardened, the outline has a clear-cut strength. The "jewels" in ornaments and crown are completely shaped in metal and are not actual gems.

25

25. Lokeshvara. Fourteenth century. Gilt copper. H: 8¹/₈˝.
The Cleveland Museum of Art, Cleveland, Ohio. Edward L. Whittemore Fund.

Bodhisattva Avalokiteshvara as Lord of the World (Lokeshvara) has many forms. None of the one hundred and eight forms known today completely agrees with this image.

26. Tara. End fourteenth century. Riveted sheet copper. H: 36˝.
Victoria and Albert Museum, London, England.

The basic feminine type evolved in seventh century sculpture (2—4) is seen here in a mode comparable to that of 16th century Venuses by Lucas Cranach. The ornaments differ from the norm but similar shapes are worn by a Bodhisattva. See Barrett, *loc. cit.*, Fig. 4.

27. Jambhala. Fourteenth century (?). Copper. H: 3¹/₄˝.
Mr. and Mrs. Aschwin Lippe, New York City.

Classical in its balanced equipoise, and reminiscent of eleventh century Pala images of Jambhala, this image of the pot-bellied God of Wealth makes of the mongoose a keenly and intimately felt animal study. The vase of plenty, spilling its contents below the foot of the god which rests on its curvature, is endowed with a life of its own.

27

31

32

**28. Nagas. Ca. seventeenth century. Gilt bronze. H: ca. 2¹/₄".
Seattle Art Museum, Seattle, Washington. Thomas D. Stimson
Memorial Collection.**

These serpent gods seem to have formed part of a *prabha-mandala*. Their
pose, gestures and expression have great subtlety. The naturalistically
modeled, pendulous cheeks of the oblong faces, treatment of the scarves
covering the shoulders, and calculated curves of the writhing bodies point
toward a later date than the one hitherto assigned to these Nagas. (Cf.
Bronzes of India and Greater India, Rhode Island School of Design [Provi-
dence, Rhode Island, 1955], pp. 18, 20.)

**29. Navatmaka Heruka. Seventeenth-eighteenth century. Bronze.
H: 9¹/₂".
Mr. Alfonso Ossorio, East Hampton, New York.**

This fierce Buddha-manifestation, dances in union with his partner (*prajna*)
Nairatma ("Without-selfhood") on the Hindu gods Brahma, Indra,
Vishnu, and Shiva. On his left, he holds within the circle of his sixteen
hands the divinities of Earth, Water, Air, Fire, Moon, Sun, Death (*Yama*),
and Wealth (*Dhanada*), and on his right their animal mounts: elephant,
horse, donkey, cow, camel, man, bitch, and jackal. Nairatma ecstatically
raises her chopper and skull-bowl toward Heruka's four faces while his
front face looks at her with frenzy and compassion. The tenderness of the
full face burgeons below the coagulated flames of the crown and the
"Face of Glory" (*Kirttimukha*) above it. The expressive and almost naturalistically modeled faces, the easy postures of the four trampled Maras, the
crude and sketchy modeling of the bodies of the protagonists, all these
conflicting traits are unified by the outburst of sheer plastic power. The
image is crystallized into a structural form saturated with the fury of
Heruka. Navatmaka Heruka is described in the *Nishpannayogavali* (cf.
Gaekwad's *Oriental Series*, vol. CIX, p. 20).

**30. Padmapani Avalokiteshvara. Fifteenth century. Gilt bronze.
H: 43".
Victoria and Albert Museum, London, England.**

Illustrating a mannerism that was current in the 15th century, the Bodhisattva ideal has here become that of an overslim figure in the triply bent
stance (*tribhanga*). He is presented on elongated legs which, from the knee
downward, not only belie the continuity of his movements but do not
offer him firm support. Mannered and otherworldly, the body is surmounted
by a broad face which is not integrated into the whole image.

**31. Manjuvara. Fifteenth century. Bronze. H: 8⁷/₁₆".
Lent anonymously.**

The strong, high, lotus stalk underscores the height and stance of the Bodhisattva. The face is painted with gold and colors. (Cf. 45.)

32. Indra. Fifteenth century. Gilt bronze. H: 3³/₄″.
The Cleveland Museum of Art, Cleveland, Ohio. Anonymous gift.

Seated in the posture *sukhasana*, body and head with their triple bend (*tribhanga*), the left arm supporting the figure behind the left thigh, the right arm forming a bridge to the right knee, the figurine fills the space cone rising from its lotus base. Its modeling is similar to that of an image of Vasudhara dated 1467 (Barrett, *op. cit.*, p. 91, Fig. 2). Crown and ornaments of this debonair figurine are studded with gems.

34

33. Indra. Fifteenth century. Gilt copper repoussé. H: 10″.
University Museum, Philadelphia, Pennsylvania.

Indra, Lord of the gods, is here seated in adamantine pose, his open hands stretched out horizontally. According to a local legend, Indra came to earth and stole flowers which his mother in heaven required for a *puja* (worship). He was caught. In a shroud of mist the mother of Indra took him back to heaven. The open arms show that thenceforth Indra does not steal.

34. Indra. Fifteenth century (?). Gilt copper. H: 5″.
Brooklyn Museum, New York.

The image is unusual in the hour-glass-like stylization of its body, and the shape of the flowers. The one on the left resembles a *Vishva-vajra*. Its central part, with the seed or stamen shapes projecting from a bell-like container, recalls the object held in the right hand of Vajrapani (5).

36

35. Arapacana Manjusri. Fifteenth century. Gilt bronze. H: 3³/₄″.
Caroline and Erwin D. Swann, New York City.

Kneeling on his left knee, supporting himself on his bent right leg, the Bodhisattva brandishes the sword of discriminating knowledge while the left hand shows the gesture of exposition. At the same time fluttering scarves steady and enhance the movement. The image is inset with turquoise and spinel rubies.

36. Bodhisattva. Fifteenth century (?). Wood. H: 22″.
Mrs. Edgar J. Stone, Toronto, Ontario, Canada.

37. Lakshminarayana. Late fifteenth century. Gilt copper. H: 3⁷/₈″.
Mr. J. J. Klejman, New York City.

This conjoint figure of Vishnu and Lakshmi carries into the asymmetry of the face its bi-sexual character.

37

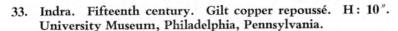

39

38. **Vajrapani. Late fifteenth century. Copper gilt. H : 8″.
The British Museum, London, England.**

The slender and contemplative Bodhisattva type is here given robustness.
Buddha Akshobhya, as spiritual father of the Bodhisattva, is seen on the
central crest of the crown of this Bodhisattva "Thunderbolt in Hand."
The crests of the crown bend inward at the top. Published: Barrett,
op. cit. p. 95, Fig. 7.

39. **Tara. End of fifteenth century. Gilt bronze. H : 28″.
The Newark Museum, Newark, New Jersey. Albert L. Shelton
Collection.**

This figure of Tara is one of the few images preserved with its *prabha-
mandala* or "surrounding effulgence," which has the shape of the back of
a throne. In its preciosity it brings up to date in physiognomy, coiffure,
and ornaments the Nepali image of the goddess (3, 4). The upper and lower
garments overlay the modeling of the figure with insistent patterns of
parallel lines, those of the lower garment being raised in double ridges.
Below the crossbar the *prabha-mandala* is astir with the frolic of bird
people (*kinnaras*) and serpentine convolutions, and, above it, with the
agitation of the ocean of air. Its currents have condensed into the shapes
of the sea monster (*makara*) and serpent-damsels (*naginis*) with Garuda
the sun-bird on top. The outer border is set with flames. An ornamental
bar at the bottom is part of the *prabha-mandala*. The pedestal is
architectural.

40. **Consort of Vrisha-Samvara. Ca. late fifteenth century. Copper.
H : 14¹/₂″.
Nepal Museum, Katmandu, Nepal.**

This female figure has to be imagined in the embrace of a bull-headed
god (Vrisha-Samvara) with whom she was united (*yuganaddha*). Her front
view would not have been visible, as she was held against the body of
the god. The figure holds the skull-bowl and chopper; her three
eyes are dilated in demoniacal frenzy; her tongue, stuck out, touches
her nose. She wears "human bone" ornaments shaped as head festoons
and skulls.

42

41. **Krishna. Fifteenth-sixteenth century. Gilt bronze. H : 6³/₄″.
Collection of Nasli and Alice Heeramaneck, New York City.**

This image of Krishna playing a flute is a work of pure Newari inspiration
created on a base of Indian iconography.

136

42. Shadakshari Mahavidya (?). Fifteenth-sixteenth century. Gilt copper. H: 7".
Collection of Nasli and Alice Heeramaneck, New York City.

In this image, figure and *prabha-mandala* form a unit; a recess in this repoussé throne partly houses the figure. Its mass is the pivot of the centrifugal and return movement of the embossed *leogryphs*, *makaras*, *nagas*, acolytes, and scrolls, strengthened by the sun-bird (Garuda) on top of the stele. The slight inclination of the head of the goddess draws the symmetry of her shape into the commotion of the total form.

43. Vina. Fifteenth-sixteenth century. Gilt copper. H: 3⁹/₁₆".
Lent anonymously.

The figure personifies the music of the Vina. She is one of the sixteen attendant goddesses of worship, which requires music, dance, incense, garland, flowers—altogether sixteen ritual ingredients. Published: *Philadelphia Museum of Art Bulletin, op. cit.* p. 27.

43

44. Bull. Fifteenth-sixteenth century. Bronze, traces of gold leaf. H: 2³/₄".
Mr. John Warrington, Cincinnati, Ohio.

Published: *The Art of Greater India*, Los Angeles County Museum, (Los Angeles, California, 1950) p. 87, No. 144; *Master Bronzes*, Albright Art Gallery, (Buffalo, New York, 1937) No. 109.

45. Manjuvara. Ca. 1500. Gilt copper. H: 4".
The Cleveland Museum of Art, Cleveland, Ohio. Gift of Margaret F. Markus in memory of her mother, Dorothy Frost Wheeler.

A form of Bodhisattva Manjusri which does not hold the sword but carries the Book, the *Prajnaparamita*, and instructs, as is shown by the hands touching in *dharmacakra mudra*.

46. Vasudhara. Beginning sixteenth century. Gilt copper, inlaid. H: 6³/₈".
The Cleveland Museum of Art, Cleveland, Ohio. Purchase from the J. H. Wade Fund.

This iconographically complete image gives to the goddess an opulent body whose proportions differ from those of the earlier images (15, 23) although all of them conform with the iconometric prescriptions, which were elastic enough to accommodate changes of style.

45

47. Ucchushma Jambhala and Vasudhara. Early sixteenth century. Copper gilt. H: 1⁵/₈″.
Mr. E. M. Scratton, Oxford, England.

A miniature group of the god of wealth and his consort shows the divinities in their fierce mood, seated on an oval lotus pedestal. This sculpture in the round is not without an admixture of drollery. The god, as prescribed, "appears as a child of five years"; he is a gnome, nude but for his snake ornaments. He holds a mongoose which vomits jewels (a ruby is inset) and in his right hand a lemon. Vasudhara holds ears of corn; her right hand bestows boons.

48. Prabha-mandala. Sixteenth century. Gilt copper. H: 12¹/₈″.
The Newark Museum, Newark, New Jersey. Golden Anniversary gift of a group of present and past staff members, 1959.

This repoussé "enclosing effulgence" (see also 39, 42) was set behind an image. The symbolism of the throne is here complete. The elephant, symbol of Earth, the Sardula or *leogryph* (the active power of the sun) in the mid-region (*antariksha*) or air, are separated by the crossbar from the Makara, here symbolizing the celestial waters. The sun-bird Garuda is at the apex, flanked by Devaputras. Scroll and flame borders edge the *prabha-mandala*.

49

49. Sarvabuddhadakini. Sixteenth century. Gilt copper. H: 13¹/₄″.
Lent anonymously.

The "Dakini of all the Buddhas," the force of inspirational consciousness, urges all the Buddhas toward the realization of Buddhahood. She strides on two prostrate, four-armed gods whose upper hands salute her. She is naked but for a garland of skulls and her jewelry. With insatiable elation she drinks blood from the foaming skull-cup in her left hand. In her right she clasps a chopper. The blood-filled skull-cup (*kapala*) does away with all ideas of substance and non-substance, and is a symbol of oneness. Published: *Philadelphia Museum of Art Bulletin, op. cit.*, p. 28.

50. Tara. Sixteenth century. Bronze. H: 5″.
The Ashmolean Museum, Oxford, England.

In this image are combined an exceptionally free posture and fleshy modeling. Published: A. K. Coomaraswamy, "Indian Bronzes," *Burlington Magazine*, May 1910, Pl. I, 4.

51. Lokeshvara. Sixteenth century. Gilt copper. H: 9¹/₈″.
William H. Wolff, Inc., New York City.

**52. Akshobhya. Sixteenth century. Gilt bronze. H: 7¼″.
Collection of Nasli and Alice Heeramaneck, New York City.**

Akshobhya, "the Imperturbable," who, in Nepal, is the foremost of the five-fold Buddhahood, is shown with the gesture of touching the earth. By this gesture Buddha Shakyamuni, called earth to witness his illumination and the defeat of Mara, the Evil one. In this image the imperturbable nature of the Buddha, the unchangeableness of the Buddha principle, the adamantine state of being beyond becoming have been given form.

**53. Vasya-Vajravarahi. Sixteenth century (?). Dry Lacquer. H: 25″.
The Cleveland Museum of Art, Cleveland, Ohio.**

Vajravarahi dances in *ardhaparyanka* posture; but for the ritual ornaments of human bone, the garland of severed heads and other ornaments—the bracelets are of metal—she is naked. A subtly horrendous smile plays over her broad face with its delicate features and dilated eyes. Although most of the attributes are lost and the left hand is missing, it appears that she held a chopper (*kartri*) in her raised and threatening right hand. This form of Vajravarahi is invoked in rituals which are performed with the purpose of bewitching men and women. Traces of red pigment show on the weathered, clay-colored surface. The material points to an earlier date than the style of the image. (Cf. P. Pelliot, "Statue en Laque Sèche dans l'Ancien Art Chinois," *Journal Asiatique*, 1923, p. 193f.)

**54. Uddiyana Kurukulla. Sixteenth century. Gilt copper. H: 7¼″.
Mr. John Warrington, Cincinnati, Ohio.**

The name of this form of Kurukulla points to Uddiyana in East Bengal, one of the original centers of Tantrik Buddhism. The goddess dances on a corpse (now missing); her main arms are engaged in drawing a flowery bow charged with an arrow of red lotus. Her second right hand held a goad of flowers; her second left hand holds a flower. Her face is fierce—five skulls are on her diadem and she wears a garland of severed heads. She bewitches and subdues men, women, ministers, and kings. Her spell-casting presence makes her hair rise like flames. The upper garment is massed and tied so as to enhance the nakedness of her body and she wears a tiger skin round her loins. Published: *The Art of Greater India*, *op. cit.*, p. 87, No. 145.

**55. Indra. Sixteenth-seventeenth century. Copper gilt, repousse. H: 11″.
Lent anonymously.**

The solemn meditation of the image is carried in vaulted shapes broadly massed in a fluid continuity of opulent curves. Its ambience is enlarged by the pendant leg of the posture, called *lalitasana*. Spinel rubies, rock crystal and emeralds enliven crown and ornaments.

51

56

56. **Adibuddha Vajrasattva. Early seventeenth century. Gilt copper. H: 5³/₄″.**
Mr. Donal Hord, San Diego, California.

The primordial Buddha in his body of bliss (*sambhogakaya*) is here shown in the graceful posture of a Bodhisattva and wearing a Bodhisattva's princely ornaments.

57. **Plaque from a ritual apron. Sixteenth-seventeenth century. Carved human bone. H: 6⁵/₈″; W: 1³/₄″.**
Dr. and Mrs. Samuel Eilenberg, New York City.

The image of Samvara, supported on a lotus and two recumbent figures, is accompanied by dancers, musicians and worshippers in two rows at the bottom. The image is flanked by pillars with lotus capitals. Above are *kinnaras*, Garuda, and *nagas*, the five Buddhas and a stupa at the top.

58. **Indra. Seventeenth century. Copper gilt. H: 3⁵/₈″.**
Dr. and Mrs. Samuel Eilenberg, New York City.

59. **White Tara. Seventeenth century. Gilt copper. H: 5¹/₄″.**
Mrs. James Marshall Plumer, Ann Arbor, Michigan.

60. **Arapacana Manjusri. Mongolia (?). Seventeenth century. Bronze. H: 5″.**
Mr. E. M. Scratton, Oxford, England.

61. **Bhairava (?). Tibet, seventeenth century. Copper. H: 4″.**
Victoria and Albert Museum, London, England.

In the transmission of sculptured types from Nepal to Tibet (such as 40) they acquire an abruptness and ruggedness, their curvilinear fluidity giving way to angularity. The mask of this male figure of fearsome (*krodha*) aspect is almost the same as that of a Nepali Bhairava.

58

62. **Padmapani. Seventeenth century. Wood. H: 6″.**
The Metropolitan Museum of Art, New York City. Rogers Fund, 1947.

Traces of the original polychromy and gilding, as on this delicately carved image, are rarely found on wood carvings more than a century old because of the custom of repainting the images.

63. **Buddha Sheltered by a Serpent. Seventeenth century. Crystal. H : 5¹/₈″.**
Cincinnati Art Museum, Cincinnati, Ohio. The William T. and Louise Taft Collection.

Seated in adamantine posture, his right hand raised in front of his chest, assuring freedom from fear, the Buddha is surmounted by the triple hood of the Serpent whose body is his support. It rests on a base suggestive both of rocks and lotus petals. The Serpent king, Mucalinda, protected the Buddha after his enlightenment, during a terrific storm. He offered his body as a seat and spread his hood above the Buddha's head to ward off the rain. Naga Mucalinda is generally represented with seven hoods, protecting the seated Buddha who is engaged in meditation.

64. **Tara. Seventeenth-eighteenth century. Wood. H : 12¹/₂″.**
Mr. and Mrs. Aschwin Lippe, New York City.

The polychromy of this image is red and white.

65. **White Tara. Eighteenth century. Gilt copper repoussé. H : 22¹/₂″.**
M. H. de Young Memorial Museum, San Francisco, California.
Avery Brundage Collection.

The repoussé technique resorted to in images of larger size, has here lent itself to splendors of modeling and ornamentation, the one enhancing the other. The lotus base is missing.

66. **White Tara. Eighteenth century. Gilt copper repoussé. H : 22″.**
Mr. J. J. Klejman, New York City.

More reticent in modeling and decoration than 65, is this repoussé sculpture of the same goddess. She is here seated in a posture of ease. Tantalizing in its slight asymmetry, her head is carried as if in a spontaneous and momentary gesture of withdrawal. The angles at which she holds her hands add expressiveness to the sign language of the *mudras*. The hip ornament below the belt, a fantasy of "green-men" and scrollwork, draws attention to this part of the body, as does, in its turn, the crown on her head. Published: K. Khandalawala, "Some Nepalese and Tibetan Bronzes," *Marg.* IV, 1958, pp. 21—40.

67. **Durga Killing the Buffalo Demon. Dated 1768. Copper gilt figure in repoussé Prabha-mandala. H : 12″.**
Lent anonymously.

Durga—here shown having sixteen arms—about to behead the Buffalo demon, strides from the lotus on the Buffalo's head to the lotus resting on her lion. This triple group, each part cast separately, is bolted together. A flaming *prabha-mandala* unites the figures. A Kirttimukha, devouring

59

serpents, appears on top. Complete images of this type were part of the "*torana*" or *supraporte*, as of the golden *torana*, dated 1619, inside the Mulchok Palace at Patan. The image was made during the rule of King Jayaprakasha Malla.

68. Samvara. Eighteenth century. Copper. H : 14″.
Lent anonymously.

This twelve-armed image, which is partly hammered and partly cast, has lost its left set of four arms which were once bolted to the body. Clad in a tiger skin, the Yidam, with knees bent, stands firmly on both legs. The hands, held in *simhamukha mudra* have lost their weapons. Crescent moon and sun appear on the high double topknot of the four-faced head. Despite the mechanization of its execution, the image is powerful and monumental.

69. Pandaravasini. Eighteenth century. Copper repoussé. H : 7³/₄″.
Lent anonymously.

This "White-clad" one (Pandaravasini), triumphant in her ecstatic detachment, is the consort or gnosis (*prajna*) of Buddha Amitabha. The figure, part of the conjoint image of Buddha "Infinite Light," originally clasped her partner in the embrace of her legs. She raises gleefully the chopper and skull-cup.

70. Varuna. China (Peking). Eighteenth century. Gilt copper. H : 4¹¹/₁₆″.
Mr. and Mrs. Richard C. Bull, Philadelphia, Pennsylvania.

The Chinese contribution to this spirited image, which was made in Peking, is seen particularly in the shape of the pedestal representing water, the element of Varuna, and that of the Makara which here has the shape of a dragon.

71. Bodhisattva. China (Peking). Eighteenth century. Copper gilt. H : 18″.
The Newark Museum, Newark, New Jersey. Gift of C. Suydam Cutting, 1950.

The flamboyant delicacy of the accoutrements and the naturalism of the feminine shape of body and face leave the eye unprepared for the heavy feet with their Chinese stylization.

72. Puja Devata. Nineteenth century. Wood. H : 22″.
Mrs. Edgar J. Stone, Toronto, Canada.

Polychrome wooden attendant figures were set up by the side of the main image during *Puja*.

73. **Standing male figure. Wood. H: 16³/₈".**
Dr. and Mrs. LeRoy Davidson, Los Angeles, California.

Figures of this kind, in metal (Nepal Museum, Katmandu) and ivory (Victoria and Albert Museum, London) adhere to an ancient type. They all have the same headdress, a high three-peaked crown and a broad coiffure, which is not known on other figures.

73

74 a. **Book covers of an Ashtasahasrika Prajnaparamita (Book of**
and **the Perfection of Wisdom). Dated 1028. Gouache on wood.**
74 b. **2¹/₂" × 17¹/₄".**
Lent anonymously.

The inner side of the wooden book covers of the palm leaf manuscripts lent themselves to longer compositions than the small squares reserved on the palm leaves, where space for illustration is found only between the lines of the text. The composition is an assemblage of groups and single figures as they would appear in the palm leaf illustrations. They are unified in this instance by the repetitive pattern of palm trees. Published: M. Mookerjee, "An Illustrated Cover of a Manuscript of the Ashtasahasrika Prajnaparamita in a Private Collection," *Lalit Kala*, No. 6 (1959) p. 53f, Plates E—G.

75. **Book cover of an Ashtasahasrika Prajnaparamita. Ca. mid-**
eleventh century. Gouache on wood. 2¹/₈" × 22".
Collection of Nasli and Alice Heeramaneck, New York City.

Single scenes illustrating the life of the Buddha are combined into one composition, though lines demarcate one scene from the next. Coarse and vivacious, these paintings combine aspects of Newari folk art with the traditions not only of the Eastern Indian school of painting but also of others. The Nepali decoration of the painted house, and the diminutive lions above the subdued elephant in rut, are of particular interest. The lions symbolize the power of Buddha, the Lion of the Shakya clan. The scene of Buddha's death shows bearded figures of a type unknown to the Pala school. These, and the rectangular compartments into which the oblong book cover (*palaka*) is divided, may be from a school of painting like that of the Indra Sabha at Ellora. Published: G. Tucci, *Tibetan Painted Scrolls*, Rome, 1949, p. 327, Pl. B.

76 detail

76. **Leaf from an Ashtasahasrika Prajnaparamita, Pala School,**
Eastern India. Late eleventh century. Gouache on palm leaf.
2¹/₄" × 17¹/₂".
Collection of Nasli and Alice Heeramaneck, New York City.

The oblong shape of the manuscript leaf is due to the shape of the palm leaf. Such leaves are perforated in two places and strung together. They are placed between two wooden planks covered with paintings on both

79 detail

sides, the figural scenes appearing only on the inner sides. One or more small square panels are reserved on the palm leaf for painting. The oblong shape is retained even when the pages are made of paper.

77 a. **Book cover and leaf from an Ashtasahasrika Prajnaparamita.**
and **Dated 1110 A.D. Cover, $2^1/_2'' \times 22^7/_{16}''$, gouache on wood. Leaf,**
77 b. **$2^3/_8'' \times 22^1/_8''$, gouache on palm leaf.**
The Cleveland Museum of Art, Cleveland, Ohio. Purchase from the J. H. Wade Fund.

The scheme of these illuminations is related to (76) whereas their style is nearer to (78) without, however, the residual modeling. Published: *The Art of Greater India*, op. cit., p. 85, No. 140.

78. **Leaves from a Gunakarandavyuha (?). Eastern Indian School.**
Twelfth century. Gouache on palm leaf. $2'' \times 21^5/_8''$.
Collection of Nasli and Alice Heeramaneck, New York City.

The swift and pliant drawing and the entire panel full of shapes and their setting differ noticeably from those where a single figure appears on the plain colored ground of its mandorla (76). The present illustration, richer in the representation of both action and setting, shows a tree and mountain fantasy modeled in color. The painted stylization of the rocks has the same Indian origin as do their sculptural versions in Nepal (III).

79. **Leaf from an Ashtasahasrika Prajnaparamita. Eastern Indian**
School. Ca. 1200. Gouache on palm leaf. $2^1/_4'' \times 18^1/_2''$.
The Detroit Institute of Arts, Detroit, Michigan.

The fluid outlines of the illuminations of this manuscript show yet another version of the Eastern Indian style, and distinguish it from Nepali work.

80. **Shivadharma. Thirteenth century. Painted book cover.**
$3^7/_8'' \times 21^3/_{16}''$.
Bir Library, Katmandu, Nepal.

On the inside of this Shaiva book cover, below the central arch of an arcade, sits Uma-Maheshvara enthroned on a rock platform with Ganesha and Karttikeya. The trefoil arch above is set with rocks and has the image of Ganga in the center. Sadhus, royal devotees, and Shiva in various aspects occupy the niches. Their ground is covered with tapestry-like scroll work. The baluster-like pillars, their shafts drawn in by an Amalaka ring, have lotus capitals. The arches are flamboyant with scrollwork and there is a Face of Glory (*kirttimukha*) at each apex. Some of the figures are modeled in light and dark tones of the same color, achieving a three-dimensional effect in front of the tapestry-like ground. Such Hindu illuminated manuscripts and bookcovers, though not as copious as the Buddhist ones are known in dated examples of the twelfth century (*Vishnu-dharma*, 1120, Bir Library, Katmandu; *Srimahamanthanabhairava-tantra*, 1180, Library of Fieldmarshal Kaiser, Katmandu).

81. Zodiacal signs and divinities. End of fourteenth or early fifteenth century. Painting on palm leaf. 4$^3/_8''$ × 10$^5/_8''$.
The Metropolitan Museum of Art, New York City. Rogers Fund, 1955.

82. Amoghapasha Avalokiteshvara. Pata. Dated: 1436. Painting on cloth. 22$^1/_2''$ × 17$^1/_2''$.
Rijksmuseum voor Volkenkunde, Leiden, The Netherlands.

The painting, according to its inscription, represents Amoghapasha of the Mahabhuta temple in Bhatgaon. The image is flanked by two goddesses, Tara and Bhrikuti on Amoghapasha's left and by two gods, Sudhanakumara and Hayagriva on the right. Flying Devaputras in flower-like, flaming, three-lobed niches, appear above on either side, next to the sun and moon. Donors are seen at bottom; palm trees behind the standing divinities; floral overall patterns within the mandala. The rest of the ground is dotted with white flowers. The purpose of the painting was to bring long life, prosperity and ample progeny to the donors. Published: P. H. Pott, "Die Kunst Tibets," in *Kunst der Welt—Burma*, *Korea*, *Tibet*. Pl. on p. 168.

83. Adi-Buddha Vajradhara. Pata. Nepali School of Nor Monastery, S. Tibet. First half fifteenth century. Painting on cloth. 33$^3/_8''$ × 31$^1/_4''$. Lent anonymously.

The primordial Buddha, he who exists from the beginning (the Buddha principle) is shown here enthroned on a lion, Kinnara, and lotus throne. Seated in adamantine pose, he holds in *vajrahumkara mudra* the *vajra*, symbol of ultimate reality, and the bell, symbol of gnosis (*prajna*). His color is blue and he is flanked on his right by the standing figure of Bodhi-sattva Ghantapani or Vajrapani. His bell and *vajra* are supported by flowers. He is flanked on his left by the Prajna who carries the skull-bowl and chopper. Below the Makara, the symbols of the throne are here elephant, lion, Kinnara, and Shardula. They are surmounted by twisting scrolls and the triple jewel at the apex. Surrounding divinities, encircled by lotus stalks, are arranged in the border. Two abbots enthroned and four goddesses help to fill the central square. Self-toned scroll work covers the dark blue ground of the central square and of the dark red throne. The salmon pink trefoil aureole of Vajradhara is left unglazed, heightening its luminosity. Ancient Chinese textile patterns decorate the loincloths of the three main figures and the cloth in the center of the throne. The drapery of the two standing figures is more Tibetan than Nepali in treatment, the *pata* having been painted in Tibet at the Nor monastery by a Nepali master or his Tibetan disciple.

84. Amoghapasha Avalokiteshvara.   Pata.   First half fifteenth century. Painting on cloth.   27″×23″.
Lent anonymously.

The Bodhisattva in his mandorla and flanked by his four attendant divinities (see 82) appears here in his temple. The upper part of this painting with the upper floors and tower is missing. Lotus-surmounted pillars support cells with Buddha images; celestials are placed one above the other in open balconies; others approach, worshipping, on lateral lotus platforms. In rectangular compartments below are shown the punishments in purgatory and other scenes; at the bottom, portraits of the donor and his very large family. The colors of this painting are mainly deep blue, Indian red, white and flesh color. Their strong contrasts set off the great delicacy of line, modeling and figural expression.

85. Traylokyavijaya (?) Pata.   Dated 1467.   Painting on cloth. 42³/₄″×27¹/₂″.
Lent anonymously.

This deity (face and body colored blue on the right, green on the left) is shown here in the embrace of his red Prajna. His eight main arms are surrounded by a circle of seventy-two additional arms arranged in two concentric semicircles, each hand holding a weapon, symbol, dismembered part of the human body, flower, skeleton, etc. The two main hands of the god embrace the Prajna with *vajra-humkara mudra*, holding thunderbolt (*vajra*) and bell. The next pair of his arms is lowered toward the gluteals in *karana hasta*. The Prajna ("sophia;" consort) ecstatically raises her right arm holding a *vajra*. The deity has seventeen heads in five tiers; the dark angry face of Vajrapani (?) surmounts the pyramid of sixteen peaceful, three-eyed faces. It is crowned by a *vishva vajra*. Legs of a flayed elephant terminate the array of hands. Two legs of the figure are raised in his dance, the other two are supported on downtrodden demoniacal creatures. The apparition of the god, in front of his aureole or "sea of flames," rests on a double lotus. Four skull-cups and four Dakinis appear on the scrollwork of the "sea of flames" of the aureoles.

The eight cemeteries are indicated, mainly by their eight guardians. They are small and arranged laterally in tiers. Yidams and a bull-headed goddess are shown in the four corners. At the bottom, Yamantaka, the Ender of Death, is in the center; the royal donor and his family are at the extreme right and left of this arcade. The name of King Ratnamalla is given in the inscription; the name of the painter is only partly legible. The inscribed date corresponds to 1467 in our calendar.

84

86. Mahakala, Protector of the Tent. Pata. Nepal school in Tibet. Fifteenth century. Painting on cloth. $38^{1}/_{4}'' \times 26^{1}/_{4}''$. Lent anonymously.

The central figure of Mahakala (the Great Black One) holds skull-bowl and chopper, symbols of severance from mortality. The chopper destroys ignorance, the skull-cup signifies absolute oneness. The god tramples on man, naked and recumbent on the large, lotus flower pedestal. Mahakala is wreathed with serpents, decked out with a tiger skin and filigree ornaments of human bone, inscribed with the sacred syllables *om ah hum* on belly and ankles. A cudgel rests in his bent arms, its ends tied with fluttering cloth. A shawl inscribed with lotus pattern and figures arches above his shoulders. The red-gold hair of the dark blue god falls in locks to his shoulders and is piled up as his crown. In the central crest of his diadem dances the miniature shape of sixteen-armed Hevajra in the embrace of his consort (*prajna*) Nairatma.

Among the four collateral images, Nilambara Vajrapani stands on the prostrate figure of Shiva and Sri Devi (Lhamo), the consort of Mahakala, "goddess of arms in a world of sensual pleasures" rides her mule over a sea of blood. The flames emanating from these blue gods rise in layered peaks of feathery scrolls. Against them are shown the dark figures of jackals, crows and Garudas, as well as other aspects of Mahakala; the one in the shape of a Brahman playing on a thighbone flute is modeled in lighter tones of blue, as is Sri Devi.

This total apparition blazes forth in the center of the eight cemeteries, symbolizing the center of the human heart. The eight cemeteries are symbolic of the annihilation of the eight propensities of the ego by which it is tied to the world. These human characteristics dwell in the heart. They are imagined as being situated in the eight directions of space where their annihilation is shown as taking place. Each of the eight directions is symbolized by its presiding divinity. Beginning from the east (at the bottom of the painting) Indra is shown on his white elephant, Shiva on his bull in the northeast, Kubera (here) on a blue horse in the north. Vayu appears on an antelope in the northwest, Varuna on the Makara (sea monster) in the west, Yama on a buffalo in the southwest, Nirriti on man in the south, and Agni on a ram in the southeast. The prescribed position of the cemeteries may be seen in a mandala (87). In this painting however, two cemeteries are painted in each of the four corners. They are peopled with scenes of torture and with Siddhas. Siddhas are perfect men, living examples of mystical realization whose presence intensifies the purifying function of the cemetery. Adi-buddha Vajradhara is shown in the center of the top row, Buddhist hierarchs and others in collateral arcades. In the bottom border Indra appears in the center, with a Buddhist monk, with Sri Devi, and further forms of Mahakala, etc.

87

87. Nairatma Mandala. Nepal school in Tibet. Ca. fifteenth century. Painting on cloth. 24″×20¹/₂″. Lent anonymously.

Nairatma, "no-self," (the embodiment of *shunya*, the Void) dances on a corpse in the center of her mandala. Scrollwork fills the ground of the central lotus, the palace-square, the surrounding circle and its outer flame edge. The eight cemeteries make lively cartouches of the central border of this circle. Siddhas and hierarchs appear in the upper border; forms of Nairatma, etc. in the lower border. In the field between mandala and borders Nairatma is united with Heruka dancing; hierarchs and others are encircled by lotus stalks. This mandala is connected with the school of the Vajradhara pata (83) but appears to be of the later part of the century.

88. Vasudhara Mandala.   Ca. 1504.   Painting on cloth.   37¹/₂″×26″. Lent anonymously.

Vasudhara is shown in the center of her mandala. For the inner border the traditional colors are used in three of the four regions—white (east), green (north), red (west)—but blue instead of yellow is used for the south; yellow, being the color of Vasudhara, is concentrated on her six-armed figure. Buddha Ratnasambhava is above her head. Above him are Jambhala, companion goddesses and attendants, *yakshas* carrying bags full of wealth, cudgels, etc. Each has his own station in the eight directions within the square. Outside the mandala are scenes illustrating the ten evil states in purgatory, and scenes from the story of Simhala. The five-fold Buddhas occupy the middle of the top row. Dancing Vighnantaka is in the center of the bottom row, flanked by the figure of the royal donor (Jayaratna-malla?) with symbols, family, and retinue. The name of this king is given in an inscribed and dated (1504) mandala of Vasudhara in the British Museum, of the same style and provenance as this one. Published: Stella Kramrisch. "Nepalese Painting," *Journal of the Indian Society of Oriental Art*, I. 1933, Calcutta, p. 129. Pls. XXXIX, XL.

89. Lokeshvara (Sukhavati?) and Tara.   Pata.   Dated 1570.   Painting on cloth.   22³/₄″×18″.
Lent anonymously.

The main god and goddess in their arched shrine, flanked by two minor divinities, are surmounted by foliate scrollwork emanating from the "Face of Glory" with its serpents at the apex. Sun and moon, together with auspicious signs in their red circles, float on the dark blue ground. At the top are the Five Buddhas; lions and donors are at the bottom. The lateral scenes illustrate a legend telling of the liberation of a fish by the seventh daughter of the man who had brought it and recounting that she went to heaven. Published: P. C. Bhagchi, "A Note on a Painted Banner," *Journal of the Indian Society of Oriental Art*, I. 1933, Pl. 1, where the deities are identified as Manjusri and Prajnaparamita; see also p. 146, ib.

90 A—C   Hitopadesha.   1594.   Folding book painted on paper.
Pages: $2\,^5/_8'' \times 8\,^3/_4''$.
Bir Library, Katmandu, Nepal.

These illustrations show the well known fable of "The Deer, the Vulture, and the Jackal." In the two upper panels of the pages illustrated here, the fable of the old vulture is recorded. He had lost his eyes and his talons; the birds who roosted in the tree provided him with food. A cat, pretending to be of an æsthetic disposition and eager to learn wisdom from the old bird, won his confidence and settled in the hollow of the tree. After devouring the nestlings of the birds and leaving their bones, the cat slipped away. The parent birds discovered the bones. Concluding that the old vulture was the culprit they pounced upon and killed him.

In the panel at the bottom, a jackal befriending a deer takes him to a field of green corn to graze there, whereupon its owner sets a trap and the deer gets caught. The jackal, who has been looking forward to feeding on the corpse of the deer, fails to get his prey which is released from the trap by the husbandman.

The oblong pages, reminiscent of manuscripts painted on palm leaves, are either filled entirely by painted scenes or the paintings are interspersed in small rectangles in the text. The background of the paintings, covered with opulent foliated scrollwork, is divided by thin verticals of the stems of trees with spreading tops of similar scrollwork. The scenes of the fables are enacted below their canopies. The sumptuous setting enriches the brisk drawings of the feral protagonists. Fierce and bristling with animation, the illustrations reproduced are nearer the level of folk art than are most of the paintings of this Hitopadesha.

91.   Siddhas, Hierarchs, etc.   Pata.   Nepal school in Tibet.   Sixteenth century.   Painting on cloth. $22\,^{11}/_{16}'' \times 19\,^3/_4''$.
The Cleveland Museum of Art, Cleveland, Ohio. Purchase from the J. H. Wade Fund.

This pata, one of a series of similar paintings, represents the work of a Nepali school in Tibet. The use of white lines delineating eyes or mouth adds an uncanny note. The figures are enthroned. Each of the two Siddhas holds a skull cup. The hierarchs belong to the spiritual lineage of Vajrapani and Manjusri respectively, as is shown by their symbols on lotuses.

92.   Vasudhara Mandala.   Sixteenth century.   Pata.   Painting on cloth. $45\,^3/_8'' \times 35\,^1/_4''$.
Collection of Nasli and Alice Heeramaneck, New York City.

Though more elaborate, this painting follows the Vasudhara mandala of 1504 in the British Museum (see 88). Here the border of the circle shows the regents of the eight directions. The names of Jayaratnamalla and Jayaindramalla are given in the inscription which also makes reference to the Kashtha *mandapa*, the resthouse for pilgrims, which has given the city of Katmandu its name. The date has been read as 1516 by W. Norman Brown and as 1555 by P. Pal. Published: *The Art of Greater India, op. cit.* p. 88, No. 146.

93. Stupa. Pata. Late sixteenth century. Painting on cloth. 37³/₄″ × 18³/₄″. National Museum of India, New Delhi, India.

The stepped central portion of the painting contains a stupa with its enclosed goddess (Ushnishavijaya), a square *harmika* with the eyes of the Adi-buddha, its *shikhara*-like top surmounted by an umbrella. Flower garlands are stretched in a triangle from the umbrella to the base. Rows upon rows of miniature stupas dot the background. The five Buddhas are seen in the top row; four donors and their many women appear in the two bottom rows. The lateral floral borders of the pata are similar to those of Pahari miniature paintings of a later date.

94 a.

94 a. Brahma and Sarasvati. Pata.   Sixteenth-seventeenth century. and   Painting on cloth.   25″ × 17¹/₂″. 94 b.   The Museum of Fine Arts, Boston, Massachusetts.

This pata is painted on both sides of the fabric. Brahma is shown on one side, four-headed and eight-handed; eight-armed Sarasvati appears on the other. Both are dancing on their *hamsa vahana* (gander), both holding trident and book in their upper hands.

95. Chakrasamvara. Pata. Sixteenth-seventeenth century. Painting on cloth.   57¹/₂″ × 32³/₁₆″. National Museum of India, New Delhi, India.

The Yidam Samvara with his Prajna Vajravarahi are supported by the downtrodden bodies of Bhairava and Kalaratri. The naturalism of their contorted shapes contrasts with the stylization of such figures in earlier paintings, just as the freer treatment of the lotus petals also differs from their formalism in an earlier Pata (85). Whereas in the earlier work the base of the group suggested a solid slab conceived in three-dimensional terms, it is here a thin plate hovering in space above the tips of the petals. The bordering figures, whether single or conjoint, embracing before the discs of their haloes and aureoles, repeat the movement of the central group and strengthen its impact.

96. Tirtha Mahatmya. Dated 1635. Painting on cloth. 15³/₈″ × 51¹/₄″. The Cleveland Museum of Art, Cleveland, Ohio. Gift of Mrs. Albert S. Ingalls.

Twelve holy places of pilgrimage are shown in the juxtaposition of green, pink, deep blue and white surfaces. The system of coloring through the use of contrasting zones is similar to Rajasthani painting of the same age. The outlines of the sparse, slender figures recall those of earlier Nepali sculptures. The fluttering scarves of some of the figures are traced in golden lines and Chinese curves on the opaque color of the ground.

94 b

97. Pata of Dharmadhatu Vagishvara. Dated 1664. Painting on cloth. 59³/₄″ × 31″.
Mrs. Sumitra Charat Ram, New Delhi, India.

In the lower half of this unusual pata, large portraits of a worshiping couple, seated on a wheeled platform drawn by horses, appear opposite the enthroned figure of the deity, which is surrounded by an effulgence. A lion crouches below the high-backed throne. Ritual objects, a stupa, and celestials emerging from clouds fill the area between the deity and his worshipers. The model of the large Chaitya (stupa) which occupies the central upper half of the painting is near the hand of the deity, which is shown in the gesture of exposition. Nimbate figures seated on cushions, and a palm tree, are seen behind the throne of Dharmadhatu Vagishvara. The god and the donors confront each other.

The Chaitya shown in the upper part of the painting holds in its dome (womb) the goddess Ushnishavijaya, flanked by two divinities. Outside the Chaitya the scene is astir with the commotion of moving the flag. It is attached to an umbrella and is shown twice—once in the process of being moved on ropes, and also installed on top of the Chaitya. The scaffolding and the unwinding of the rope are painted in detail. Small shrines with their images, workmen, musicians, and worshipers dot the red ground with their precise shapes. A second pair of donors—or the same—are portrayed at the base of the Chaitya. A third and fourth couple, inscribed with their names, are seated near the right edge of the painting at the level of the dome. The lower part of the painting with the deity and donors, and the upper part describing the flag-moving rite, are placed within a thinly outlined, upright frame, like that of a votive stele, ending with a five-fold cusped arch.

The portraits of the worshipers or donors here form part of the main field of the painting. Their physiognomies and costumes are Nepali equivalents of such elements in contemporary Mughal portraiture. The main "stele" of the painting is surrounded by rows of miniature Chaityas. Sun and moon in their spheres are superimposed in the upper corners. The row of divinities in the upper margin and that of worshipers etc. in the lower are no longer clearly recognizable.

The inscription at the very bottom has two dates; one corresponds to 1433 A.D. in the reign of Jayayakshamalla, the other, which is the date of the painting, to the year 1664 when Jayapratapamalla, King of Poets (Kavindra) ruled. Katmandu is called Yambu, its Newari name.

99 detail

98. **Vajravarahi Mandala.   Seventeenth–eighteenth century.   Painting on cloth.   41$^{1}/_{2}$″ × 28$^{1}/_{8}$″.**
National Museum of India, New Delhi, India.

In this free version of a mandala, the goddess dances on a corpse in the center of her hexagon (*shadkona*). Her companion goddesses stride in the six small triangles that reach out in star shape from the central hexagon. Vases supporting skull-bowls appear on the star-dotted circle. An inner circle of lotus petals and, on the outer side, rims of skulls and flames enclose the eight cemeteries. They are here without their horror, pleasaunces where the regents of the eight directions reside and the Siddhas sport. Their style is a revival of fifteenth century form. A parsemé ground is used outside the circle and, in between, the ancillary divinities and manifestations in their aureoles fill the surrounding square. The portraits of the donors are clad in the fashion of the day.

99. **Shiva with Avatars of Vishnu.   Eighteenth century (?).   Painting on cloth.   24$^{1}/_{2}$″ × 79$^{1}/_{2}$″.**
The Denver Art Museum, Denver, Colorado.

The mountains in Nepali style here produce a flat screen behind the figures. The undulating top of this mountain screen is capped by cloud ruffles. A fastidious rococo guides the brush of the artist whether he paints a tree, the intricacies of the throne or the man-lion incarnation of Vishnu who, having burst forth from behind a pillar, is clawing at the entrails of his adversary. From the end of the seventeenth century the pupils of the eyes, when shown in front view, were placed near the inner corners of the eyes, giving to the faces a hypnotizing stare.

100 a.
and
100 b.
Book cover and leaf from an Ashtasahasrika Prajnaparamita. Early eighteenth century. Cover, gouache on wood. Leaf, gouache on paper.   4$^{1}/_{2}$″ × 18″.
Lent anonymously.

On the cover Buddha is shown walking, carried by Naga Shesha, accompanied by monks and gods, and worshipped by a pair of donors. The illuminated page illustrates the Temptation of the Buddha.

101. **Vishnu Pata.   Ca. 1810.   Painting on cloth.   20″ × 202″.**
Bharat Kala Bhavan, Banaras Hindu University, Banaras, India.

The pata depicts the story of Kaundinya and his wife Sita, which is being told by Krishna to the five Pandavas. It relates the marriage of Kaundinya, the vow performed by his wife, the burning of Kaundinya's house, the austerities of Kaundinya in the forest, his finding of the old sage Ananta, and his worship of Vishnu. Among the figures in the lower register is that of the boy-King Girvana Yuddha Vikrama Sah (1800—1816), a devotee of Vishnu.

102. Assemblage of images. Pata. Dated 1775. Painting on cloth. 29$^1/_8$″ × 22″.
Lent anonymously.

Although cursively drawn and symmetrically coordinated, the effect of the pata is determined by the directional lines of the movements of the divinities. Each in his specific color (which is iconographically prescribed) stands out harmoniously from the red "sea of flames" around him and the deep blue and green of the pata's ground. In the center appears Yogambara with his Prajna Jnanadakini. In the top row are Kalacakra, Dharmadhatu Vagishvara and Navatmaka Heruka; in the second row Vajrahunkara and Samvara. In the third row are Yamantaka, Vighnantaka and Ubhayavarahanana. The names of members of the donor's family and the date 875 of the Newari era (A.D. 1775) are given in the inscription. (Cf. 97.)

103. The Story of Banasura. Later part of eighteenth century (?). Painting on cloth. 29$^1/_2$″ × 141$^3/_4$″.
Musée Guimet, Paris, France.

Banasura, son of Bali, king of the demons, had one thousand arms. He was a devotee of Shiva, who guarded his city. Bana was a great war lord but did not find sufficient use for his thousand arms. He complained to Shiva who foretold that soon someone who was his equal would quell his pride. The occasion came when Bana found Aniruddha, the grandson of Krishna, in the palace apartment of his daughter Usha, where he had been carried miraculously through the air by her maid. Bana made Aniruddha his prisoner. This part of the story is shown in the upper half of the long scroll. The lower half shows the battle between Krishna —flying on Garuda—and Banasura. Krishna kills the retinue of Banasura and finally chops off his arms. Now Shiva pleads for his devotee. His last pair of arms is then spared and Krishna releases Aniruddha. The three-dimensional palaces and the riffled mountain ranges form an animated stage for the briskly told narrative.

104. Navatmaka Heruka. Tanka. Tibet. Eighteenth century. Painting on cloth. 17$^1/_2$″ × 12$^1/_2$″.
Collection of Nasli and Alice Heeramaneck, New York City.

In this tanka (the Tibetan word for a temple "banner") the angularity into which the curves of the dancing figures are forced conveys an agony fiercer in its nature than the rapture expressed in Nepali patas showing the Yidams with their partners.

105. 106. **Illustrations from a Bhagavata purana. Middle of nineteenth century. Gouache on paper. $14^{1}/_{8}'' \times 20^{1}/_{2}''$.**
Lent anonymously.

Prasena possessed the Shyamantaka jewel which the sun god had presented to his brother. Krishna asked for this magical jewel. Prasena refused and took it to the forest where he was killed by a lion. The painting shows Prasena coming to the forest to hunt and being killed by the lion who then walks away with the jewel.

Jambavan, the Lord of bears, killed the lion, took the jewel and brought it to his daughter. Krishna, having followed Prasena and the tracks of Jambavan, fought with the Lord of bears, defeated him and was given by Jambavan both the jewel and his daughter. The painting shows this touching scene, Jambavan having come forth from his "palace" on the left side of the picture.

107. **Khadga (sword). L : $34^{1}/_{2}''$.**
Dr. and Mrs. Samuel Eilenberg, New York City.

Similar swords are published. (Cf. W. Egerton, *Handbook of Indian Arms*, London, 1880, Pl. IX, 350 and 352; p. 102.) Swords having a curved blade, sometimes ending in the head of an animal, were found in Ashur and are known from Babylonian representations (cf. Rachel Maxwell Hyslop, "Daggers and Swords in Western Asia," *Iraq VIII*, 1946, p. 42; Y. Yadin, *The Art of Warfare*, New York, 1963). They were used ceremonially rather than as weapons.

154

GLOSSARY names of Buddhist and Hindu gods represented in the exhibition.

Adi-buddha: The primordial Buddha; Buddhahood in itself.

Akshobhya: The Buddha "Imperturbable"; image of the power inherent in the Buddha. This power was shown by Buddha Shakyamuni when he attained enlightenment, remained steadfast under the attack, and defeated Mara, the Evil One. Akshobhya, a hypostasis of that power, seated in adamantine position, his right pendant hand pointing to the earth, is associated with the East. His symbol is the *Vajra* (thunderbolt). His color is blue. The particular human failing which finds release in him is wrath. (Cf. "Buddha.")

Amitayus: The Buddha "Boundless Life"; image of Nirvana, the state of deathlessness. Seated in adamantine position, the hands resting on his lap, palm on palm, support a vase full of the water of deathlessness. Amitayus is the "form of splendour" (*sambhogakaya*) of Buddha Amitabha, "Boundless Light". His region is the West. His symbol is the lotus flower. His color is red. (Cf. "Buddha.")

Avalokiteshvara: Bodhisattva Avalokiteshvara, "The Lord who directs his gaze downward," is the spiritual son of Buddha Amitabha. He has one hundred and eight forms. (See Bodhisattva.)

Bhairava: "The Fearful," originally a terrific (*ugra*) form of the Hindu god Shiva; wrathful but protective spirit, the emanation of divine omnipotence, slayer of demons. Nepal is the sphere of action of 5,600,000 Bhairavas.

Bodhisattva: A being who all his life strives for enlightenment (*bodhi*), which becomes his essential self. He renounces Nirvana, however, and leads a life of action in order to save mankind. Regarding the relation of Bodhisattva and Buddha, see "Buddha."

Brahma: Brahma, to the Hindu, is Deity manifested as the creator of the universe. His vehicle is the Hamsa, the celestial gander. In Tantrik-Buddhist images, Brahma is one of the four Evil Ones (Mara) trampled upon by Hevajra and other gods.

Buddha: The "Enlightened" was a sage of the royal Shakya clan (Shakyamuni). For the current æon he is the Lord Buddha. He embodies Buddhahood. In former æons other perfect and enlightened sages had taught the doctrine and in a future æon Maitreya will be the Buddha. This "historical" sequence of the appearance of a Buddha rests in the idea of Buddhahood which is timeless. The principle of Buddhahood is the Adi-buddha. This principle, when viewed as active throughout the cosmos, is represented as fivefold with reference to the central realization which is resplendent (*vairocana*) and is represented by Buddha Vairocana. Buddha Vairocana is placed at the center with reference to the other four exponents of Buddhahood. The Buddha nature permeating the entire cosmos is similarly realized in the four directions of space in four further forms, as Buddha Akshobhya in the east, Buddha Amitabha in the west, Buddha Ratnasambhava in the south, and Buddha Amoghasiddhi in the north. Each of these five Buddhas or fivefold exponents of Buddhahood is associated with an Orient, a cognizance, a color, a consort (*prajna*), a Bodhisattva or spiritual son, and even further members of his "family." With each of the Five Buddhas is also associated a particular human failing: wrath, malignity, desire, envy and stupidity. (Cf. Yidam.)

Devaputra: "Son of god," a flying celestial represented in child form.

Devata: A celestial being.

Devi: Goddess.

Garuda: The mythical Sun-bird, vehicle of Vishnu, Garuda is represented as part man, part bird.

Gauri: "The Brilliant", a name of the consort of the Hindu god Shiva. An image named Mahagauri, the Great Gauri, on which there appears an inscription of the year 1205 in Deo-Patan corresponds, in general, in the position of her hands with the images called "Gauri" in this catalogue.

Green Tara: Shyama Tara, also called Khadiravani Tara, is that aspect of Tara, (the "Savioress") which belongs to the family of Buddha Amoghasiddhi, whose color is green. (Cf. Buddha.)

Heruka: The fierce aspect of a Buddha. Each of the five Buddhas has his Heruka aspect, the Buddha nature being dual. Each Heruka also has several aspects. (Cf. Navatmaka Heruka.)

Hevajra: Heruka in union with his female partner (*prajna*).

Indra: Indra, the Hindu Lord of gods, in Tantrik Buddhism is the Buddha of one of the Six Spheres of Existence. He plays a special part in the legends, life and art of Nepal. His image, with hands extended laterally, is set up annually during the Indra Festival. His other type of representation shows him seated and similar to a Bodhisattva. His frontal eye is always shown horizontally, the third eye of other divinities being regularly placed vertically in the middle of the forehead.

Jambhala: The god of Wealth belongs to the family of Buddha Ratnasambhava whose name means "Jewel-born" and whose symbol is a jewel.

Janguli: A goddess associated with Akshobhya. She cures and prevents snake bite.

Krishna: The Hindu god, Krishna, is an avatar, (earthly manifestation or "descent") of Vishnu. Among his many deeds of valor as a young boy was his defeat of the great serpent Kaliya who lived in the river Yamuna.

Lakshmi: The Hindu goddess of prosperity, consort of Vishnu.

Lhamo: A form of Kali who is a consort of Shiva. Lhamo is one of the four "Defenders of the Law" (Dharmapala). She was armed by the gods and wears their weapons as her ornaments. She is a consort of Mahakala. Before her conversion to Buddhism she was the twin sister and wife of Yama, the god of death.

Lokeshvara: The "Lord of the World" Lokeshvara is Shiva identified with Avalokiteshvara.

Mahakala: The "Great Black One" is a defender of the Law. Originally he was a form of the Hindu god Shiva, an embodiment of "Great Time" or Eternity.

Maitreya: The Future Buddha. In the present dispensation of time he is a Bodhisattva.

Manjusri: The "Glorious Gentle One" is a Bodhisattva who belongs to the family of Buddha Vairocana; he is also attached to the family of Buddha Akshobhya or of Buddha Amitabha. He is the Creator of Nepal (see Introduction). In his fiercest manifestation he is Vajrabhairava "the Adamantine Fearful" called Yamantaka, the Ender of Death.

Maya: The measurable or "phenomenal" world. Also the name of the mother of Buddha Shakyamuni.

Nairatma: "No-self" is a fierce goddess who represents Shunya, the Void. She dances on a corpse. She belongs to the family of Buddha Akshobhya.

Navatmaka Heruka: Cf. Heruka.

Padmapani: Bodhisattva "Lotus in hand," a form of Bodhisattva Avalokiteshvara, who is the spiritual son of Buddha Amitabha.

Prajna: "Gnosis" (i. e. spiritual wisdom), the consort of a Buddha with whom he is united. In relation to her, within the state of Buddhahood, he is the means (*upaya*) and she is the end.

Prajnaparamita: "Perfection of Wisdom." She is the embodiment of the *Prajnaparamita* scripture and a form of the Supreme goddess. She belongs to the family of Buddha Aksobhya.

Puja Devata: An image of an ancillary divinity set up next to the main divinity to receive worship (*puja*).

Samvara : The Yidam Samvara is a form of Hevajra. He belongs to the family of Buddha Akshobhya. His Prajna is Vajravarahi.

Sarasvati : "Our Lady of the Waters," Hindu Goddess of Speech and consort of Brahma who was taken over by the Buddhists.

Sridhara : "The upholder of Sri," one of the varieties of the cult image of Vishnu.

Stupa : The architectural symbol of the Parinirvana (total decease) of Buddha Shakyamuni; the most sacred Buddhist monument.

Tara : The "Saviouress." As the *prajna* of Buddha Vairocana, her color is white. Her attributes are eyes on her forehead, palms, and soles. As the *prajna* of Buddha Amoghasiddhi her color is green. There are in addition, yellow, blue and red Taras, belonging to the respective Buddha families. The Saviouress is everywhere. Each of her manifestations has further sub-varieties.

Tantrik (adj.) : Referring to a class of texts called Tantra, a body of Revelation on which are laid down the rites by which Buddhahood or the realization of the Ultimate can be attained in this life.

Ucchushma Jambhala : A fierce variety of Jambhala.

Uma-Maheshvara : The Hindu god Shiva in his togetherness with his shakti (creative power) as Uma.

Vajradhara : The Adi-buddha, "Holder of the Vajra" (thunderbolt), is iconographically distinguished from Vajrasattva.

Vajrasattva : The Adi-buddha "Vajra-Being" differs from Vajradhara in the position of the hands holding the *Vajra* (thunderbolt) and *Ghanta* (bell). The *vajra* is the male symbol standing for the "means" (*upaya*), the bell, the female symbol for the doctrine (*prajna*).

Vajravarahi : The "Adamantine She-boar" belongs to Buddha Vairocana's family. She is entrancingly beautiful, being the indestructible female element of intuition, the essence of the five kinds of wisdom, the embodiment of "the *Sahaja* pleasure". Her attribute is an excrescence on the left side of her head, which has the shape of the head of a boar.

Varuna : The Regent of the West. His mount is the Makara (sea monster).

Vasudhara : The "Giver of Wealth" (the Earth), belongs to the family of Buddha Ratnasambhava and is the consort of Jambhala. Her attribute: ears of corn.

Vidyadhara : Carrier of magic knowledge, or spells, a class of celestials always represented flying.

Vikranta Murti : Vishnu in his manifestation or "descent" (*avatar*) as a tiny brahman boy who pervades the cosmos in three strides, stepping out from the piece of land—just enough to stand on—that he had begged the Demon King to give him.

Vishnu : The "Pervader", one of the three Hindu Demiurges (Brahma, Vishnu, Shiva). He preserves and restores the universe. He descends (*avatarati*) from his transcendental state in order to restore the world when, because of all the evil in it, it is threatened with destruction.

Yidam : The "Yidams" are of essential importance to the practising Tantrik Buddhist. As chosen divinities they are guarantors to the worshipper of his union in Buddhahood with the particular one of the five Buddhas to whom he is markedly drawn by that human failing to which he is most prone. His failing may be wrath, malignity, desire, envy, or stupidity. Contrasting with the serenity of the "Buddha image" is its fierce, Heruka form. Through the divine mechanism of these Heruka-Yidams the failing of the practiser is transmuted into that special kind of wisdom represented by the particular Buddha. Thus there developed the fierce forms of Akshobhya and the different forms of Heruka, Hevajra, Samvara, etc. (Cf. Buddha.)

107. Khadga (sword). L : 34½″.

SHORT BIBLIOGRAPHY

Barrett, D., "The Buddhist Art of Tibet and Nepal," *Oriental Art*, 1957, p. 90f.

Bhattacharyya, B. B., *The Indian Buddhist Iconography*. Calcutta, 1958.

Bhattacharyya, B. B., (ed.) *Nishpannayogavali*. Baroda, 1945.

Bhattacharyya, B. B., (ed.) *Sadhanamala*, Vols. I and II, Gaekwad's *Oriental Series*. Baroda, 1925, 1928.

Brough, J., "Legends of Khotan and Nepal," *Bulletin of the School of Oriental and African Studies*, London XII, Pt. I, p. 333 f.

Bruhl, O. Monod, "Une Peinture Nepalaise au Musée Guimet," *Arts Asiatiques*, 18, 1955, p. 297f.

Chandra, Moti, "A Painted Scroll from Nepal," *Bulletin of the Prince of Wales Museum*, I, 1955, p. 6.

Clark, W. E., *Two Lamaistic Pantheons*. Cambridge, 1937.

Coomaraswamy, A. K., *History of Indian and Indonesian Art*, New York, 1927, pp. 141—146.

Foucher, A., *Etude sur l'Iconographie Bouddhique de l'Inde*. Paris 1900.

Furer-Haimendorf, C. V., "Elements of Newar Social Structure," *Journal of the Royal Anthropological Institute*, LXXXVI, p. 15.

Gnoli, R., *Nepalese Inscriptions in Gupta Characters*. Rome, 1956.

Goetz, H., "Early Indian Sculptures from Nepal," *Artibus Asiae*, 78, 1955, p. 61.

Goetz, H., "Arte del Nepal," *Le Civilta dell'Oriente*, IV, Roma, 1962.

Khandalawala, K., "Nepalese and Tibetan Bronzes," *Marg*, IV, p. 21f.

Kramrisch, Stella, "Nepalese Painting," *Journal of the Indian Society of Oriental Art*, I, 1933, p. 129f.

Lalou, M., *Iconographie des Etoffes Peintes (pata) dans le Manjusrimulakalpa*. Paris, 1930.

Landon, Perceval, *Nepal*, 2 vols. London, 1928.

Levi, Sylvain, *Le Nepal*, Vols. I-III. Paris, 1905, 1908.

Lippe, Aschwin, "Vishnu's Conch in Nepal," *Oriental Art*, New Series VIII - 3 (Autumn, 1962) p. 2.

Lobsinger-Dellenbach, M., *Nepal: Catalogue de la Collection du Musée de Genève*, 1954.

Petech, L., *Mediaeval History of Nepal*. Rome, 1958.

Pott, P. H., *Introduction to the Tibetan Collection of the National Museum of Ethnology*. Leiden, 1951.

Pott, P. H., *The Tibetan and Nepalese Collection of the Baroda Museum*, IX, 1952—1953, p. 1f.

Regmi, D. L., *Ancient Nepal*. Calcutta, 1960.

Snellgrove, D. L., *Buddhist Himalaya*. Oxford, 1957.

Snellgrove, D. L., "Shrines and Temples of Nepal," *Arts Asiatiques*, VIII, 1961, pp. 3f., 93f.

Tucci, G., *The Theory and Practice of the Mandala*. London, 1961.

Tucci, G., *Tibetan Painted Scrolls*, 3 vols. Rome, 1949.

Walsh, E. E., "The Coinage of Nepal," *Journal of the Royal Asiatic Society of Great Britain and Ireland*, London 1908, p. 755.

Wright, Daniel, *History of Nepal*. Cambridge, 1877.

The following photographs are by Otto E. Nelson:
2, 8, 11, 15, 17, 20 (in color), 22, 33, 35, 40, 41, 42, 43, 49, 52, 53, 55, 57, 58, 64, 67, 68, 69, 70, 74, 75, 76, 79, 80, 83, 84, 85, 86 (in color), 87, 88 (in color), 89, 90 (in color), 92, 100, 102, 104, 105, 106, 107.

The color photograph No. 65 is by William Abbenseth.

Catalogue designed by Virginia Field, Assistant Director, Asia House Gallery.